Dedication

As we go through life, we pick up bits and pieces of who we are from our loved ones and friends. God places people in our lives who can help Him help us become the kind of people He calls us to be. We can take from circumstances—both good and bad—whatever we choose to take with us. We can forgive the people in our lives who hurt us. We hope that those we hurt will forgive us. In forgiveness, as Christ showed us long ago, there is tremendous power—power to love, triumph, and sustain; power to have joy, peace, and comfort; power to be strong and eventually reach our ultimate victory with Him.

I would like to dedicate this book to Mom, Dad, Doug, Matt, Luke, Del, John, Grandma Vi, David, Pam, April, Skye, Susan, Randy, Heidi, Jenni, Aimee, Amber, Peg, Jim, Donovan, Tanner, Joe, Jane, Barry, Ben, Jon, Steve, Kent, Julie, my aunts, uncles, cousins, Carol, Pam, Jackie, Barbra, Carolyn, and Patti—thank you for helping me to keep reaching to be who He's called me to be!

Most importantly, thank you to Him who loves us enough to make us truly whole!

Love,

Contents

Foreword
by H. Norman Wright

A flood of resources has been published in the past decade focusing on various types of dysfunction. Many have been helpful and enlightening. But with so many on the market, can yet another book say anything new?

Yes, it can—and this is the book which does exactly that. In a simple and yet penetrating manner, the author invites us to join a family in the intimacy of their family counseling session. You are able to see behind the scenes, and feel the interactions of a dysfunctional family. And through this approach, you gain understanding and insights that are usually undiscovered. The author is able to express both the pain which so many families experience and the hope which so many are seeking.

The author shows a sensitive understanding of the struggles of adult children of alcoholics and the process of family interaction. Whether your family situation is similar or not, you will be able to respond in a new way to yourself and to others because of spending time with this family in their personal journeys in therapy. You will be able to say, "Now I understand. It finally makes sense."

This practical book will be welcomed by anyone coming from or currently experiencing a dysfunctional relationship, as well as by those in a helping profession.

> H. Norman Wright
> Family Counseling and Enrichment Center
> Tustin, California

Letter to the Reader

When I began this book it was only going to be for the Adult Children of Alcoholics (ACOAs). But as I talked with alcoholics (drinking and sober) and their spouses, adult children, extended families, friends, employers and the professionals who work with all of them, I became aware that I couldn't truly address the complete healing of one group living with the effects of alcoholism without speaking to the entire family network involved.

This network is so tightly knit, that in order for one member to totally recover his/her whole, healthy personality, he/she must look at the others involved in the family and come to some sort of understanding and acceptance of them. This book is to help those who are caught in the alcoholic family network to identify, confront and cope with the special problems they face.

There is an insidiousness about alcoholism that seems to invade every nook and cranny of the lives it touches. The consequences of a great-grandfather's alcoholism can ripple through generations to influence a great-granddaughter in choosing the man she marries. And a great-grandson may become an alcoholic without knowing that he was predisposed to the disease.

To be really free from negative effects of the alcoholic family network, I found, during my own recovery as an ACOA, that a person goes through a five-stage process:

1. Identifying the fact that there *are* problems in your life that stem from the alcoholic family network.
2. Examining what these problems are.
3. Recognizing why you believe, act or feel as you do.
4. Reconciling yourself to the need of changing destructive behavior and belief patterns into constructive ones.
5. Restoring your original, healthy personality.

This may sound impossible. It isn't. Not only is it possible to complete the adventure, it is possible to do so in a *big* way! You can turn the negative effects of alcoholism into avenues to make you happier, healthier, stronger and more successful. Instead of using great amounts of energy just to survive, you can change those effects into wonderful, electrical energy to help you in everything from achieving physical fitness to financial fulfillment!

All you need to do is believe—even if it's only long enough to get through the pages of this book at first—and the seeds of your faith will start growing from there! In Mark 4:26, 27 Jesus says, "This is what the kingdom of God is like. A man scatters seed on the ground. Night and day, whether he sleeps or gets up, the seed sprouts and grows, though he does not know how."

As you read this book, as you talk with others about living with the effects of alcoholism and as you communicate with yourself, you will be scattering seeds of recovery in your life. In fact, your restoration process may seem to take on a life of its own, and your faith—that you can totally heal—will grow.

How magnificent! In Matt. 17:20 Jesus says, "I tell you the truth, if you have faith as small as a mustard seed, you can say to this mountain, 'Move from here to there' and it will move. Nothing will be impossible for you."

It doesn't matter how far along you are in the five stages of becoming a healthier, happier person because there are no time limits, competitions or restrictions—you can always go further and become better!

When I reached 404 names, I stopped listing the names of the people I've talked to and observed in researching this book! I didn't even attempt to keep track of the hundreds more I've read or been told about.

I am forever grateful to those who trusted me by sharing their hearts, agonies and triumphs. In order to include at least part of all the invaluable information they've honored me with, I have combined true-life experiences into one family's counseling process.

Many of their feelings and challenges may be familiar to you. It is essential that, from the beginning of your journey through this book, you try to accept and take comfort in the fact that families affected by alcoholism are very much alike in a multitude of ways. Actually, *all* dysfunctional families are alike in a great number of ways. There doesn't have to be the literal presence of alcohol or other drugs in your life to make this book meaningful to you. If an entire family seems to revolve around any one member, it is dysfunctional to some degree.

There is a source of unfailing help—beyond the corridors of pain and ugliness—for reconciling your mind, body and soul with life. This source is God.

If there is, or has been, alcoholism present in your life, you've probably heard that to depend on God is to be weak or irresponsible for your own actions. Wrong! Talk to most sober alcoholics or recovered family members and you'll find that it is just the opposite! To have the courage and strength to put God at the center of your life—to put faith in something you can't necessarily see with your eyes or feel with your hands—takes a lot of guts, especially if you are someone who has been bruised and battered by the effects of alcoholism.

My prayer for all of you who have lived or are still living in an alcoholic family network is that you will find the promise of Phil. 4:7 fulfilled in your life: "The peace of God, which transcends all understanding, will guard your hearts and your minds in Christ Jesus."

In His love,

Karen J. Sandvig

Stage 1

IDENTIFICATION

There most likely *are* problems in your life that stem from
living in an alcoholic family network.

Monarchs to the Light

Gloria Howe read over the evaluation sheet on the desk in front of her. Judge Harris had ordered the Martin family to attend group therapy and had given them a list of several mental health facilities to choose from. They had picked the Christian Treatment Center where Gloria was a counselor.

Mr. Martin, the father, had been charged with public intoxication recently after being stopped by local police as he swayed and loudly sang his way down the main street of their small New England town after midnight.

Everyone pretty much knows everyone else in small towns in New England—just as they do in the rest of the east, the north, south and west. Gloria was sure Judge Harris knew the family's background and had referred them to treatment centers in her city nearby to get professional help for what looked to her experienced eye to be an alcoholic family network.

As she glanced over some of the judge's sketchy

notes, she heard a group of people come into the building and pause collectively outside her door. She smiled as a male voice said, "Can't we just *tell* the judge we went to counseling?"

Gloria responded in a loud voice, "Sorry, that won't work—come on in, Family Martin!" The door opened slowly and a young man in his twenties peeked around the corner, grinning sheepishly. Gloria motioned for him to lead the group inside and surveyed them as they took seats on the chairs and sofa around a coffee table. Something was amiss. She glanced down at her papers and saw what was wrong—there should be six people here. It didn't surprise Gloria that two family members weren't there. In fact, she was pleased to start out with this much of the network present.

"Good evening," Gloria smiled at the Martins warmly. "I am Gloria Howe, your counselor for the next eight weeks. During our counseling sessions, we will be discussing the five stages of full recovery for members of the alcoholic family network. I'd like to start by giving you each a pamphlet to read at home that lists and describes each stage. I use this to introduce my clients to some of the things we'll explore together and a few things you may be wondering about." (See Appendix A for the pamphlet Gloria gave the Martins.)

"Wait a minute, lady!" Mr. Martin exclaimed. "Just what do you mean by 'full recovery for alcoholic family networks'? I think we're in the wrong class here! We don't need any recovering from alcoholism—or anything else!"

The air was heavy with tension as the other Martins held their breath to see how Gloria would handle their husband and father.

Gloria looked at Mr. Martin with a level gaze and said

evenly, "First of all, sir, you are not in a class—you are in family counseling because there have been problems in your life which Judge Harris feels stem from alcohol. Second, I can assure you that you are definitely in the right place."

Mr. Martin sniffed angrily and challenged Gloria with a hostile stare. Gloria continued calmly, "I understand that you may not think recovery for the alcoholic family network applies to you. Please try to bear with me for a little while and see what happens in our sessions. You may be surprised to find that we'll discuss things you really do identify with.

"If it's acceptable to you, I'd like us all to be on a first-name basis." Heads nodded nervously. Gloria took a seat in a comfortable chair facing the Martins and continued, "Well, then, why don't we start by each of you introducing and telling a little about yourself?"

All four Martins slumped a little lower in their seats—no one wanted to be first. Gloria helped things along by looking at the young man who had spoken outside her door. "How 'bout you?"

"Uh, well, okay. I'm Rod. I'm 25 and the youngest of the family. I work as a staff writer for our local newspaper and I date occasionally."

Gloria grinned. She thought she'd like Rod's sense of humor. "Thanks, Rod. Nice to meet you," she said and turned to the young woman sitting next to Rod on the sofa. "And may I make your acquaintance, please?"

"Sure!" was the enthusiastic reply. "I'm Jill. I'm 35, the oldest of our family. I have two children—12 and 13 years old—and I've just been through a lousy divorce from an alcoholic husband!" Jill crossed her arms across her chest firmly as if to say, "So there! What do you make of that?"

Gloria simply nodded her head calmly and looked to the

middle-aged couple sitting on the love seat together. "And would you be Mrs. Martin?"

"Yes. Call me Nora," the woman said congenially. She was wringing a tissue around and around her hands in her lap. She reminded Gloria of a frightened child. Gloria asked gently, "And what is your place in the family, Nora?"

Nora's eyes opened wide and she laughed anxiously. "Well, wife and mother, of course!"

"Of course," Gloria replied softly. "And Mr. Martin? Will you tell me something about yourself?"

Mr. Martin sat up stiffly and cleared his throat. "My name's Mike," he said gruffly. "I guess I'm the reason we're here. But don't think there's anything wrong in our family. I just had a little too much to drink one night and the judge didn't want to make me spend any time in jail so he had us come here instead. And as far as I'm concerned, they've carried these drinking laws way too far! A guy can't even enjoy himself anymore without the cops breathing down his neck." Mike sat back into the love seat as if to indicate he'd said all he intended to say.

Gloria looked at him for a moment, then at each of the others. She noted that Rod squirmed uncomfortably. Jill had what looked like a sneer on her face. And Nora just stared in the direction of the desk across the room. Gloria said quietly, "Nora, I see by my notes that there are two of your family members not here. Can you tell me a little about them and why they couldn't come tonight?"

"Those are our two middle children—Cole and Melanie. Cole's 31 and Melanie's 28," Nora started.

Mike interrupted. "They didn't come because they didn't want to. They don't believe in all this group counseling baloney—and I don't either!"

Gloria looked Mike straight in the eyes and said calmly, "Mike, I can appreciate your feelings about the counseling and the feelings of your other two children, but I'm sure Judge Harris had a good reason for advising your whole family to come for group therapy. I'd be grateful if you'd ask Cole and Melanie to be here for the other seven sessions."

Jill spoke up, "Cole might come, but it'll be tough to get Melanie to give up a night to be here—her social life is too important to her!"

Gloria looked at Jill. "Oh? Well, if you'll give me her phone number, maybe I can give her a call myself during this next week and ask her to come."

"No, no, no," Mike said, "I'll call her. She'll come if I ask her."

"Ha!" Jill laughed.

Mike leaned forward with an angry look. Nora quickly put a hand on his knee and he sat back in a pout. Jill looked self-satisfied. Rod glanced at Gloria and rolled his eyes with resignation.

Gloria looked at Mike and asked smoothly, "Are you an alcoholic?"

Mike sputtered in surprise. "*Of course* I'm not an alcoholic!"

Gloria turned to Nora. "Do you feel Mike is an alcoholic?"

Nora looked at her husband tensely. "Uh, well, no, I don't think so."

"You don't *think* so? Nora! Don't give this lady any funny ideas that I'm some old souse!" Mike said loudly.

Gloria ignored him and turned to Jill. "Do you think your dad is an alcoholic?"

Jill's face reddened. She looked down, and then up, then at her parents and finally at Gloria. "Maybe."

Mike's mouth fell open in astonishment. "I'll be hanged! Jill, what are you talking about?"

Jill's emotions were at the surface and her voice became childlike as she responded, "Well, Daddy, let's face it—we're not exactly teetotalers! Your mom was an alcoholic and Mom's grandfather was an alcoholic and there's Melanie—"

"Don't you bring up your sister when she's not here to defend herself!" Mike shot back. "And my mother was *not* an alcoholic! She just needed to have her brandy because of her health—you know that!"

Jill looked exasperated and gave in as quickly as she'd stepped forward. "All right, Daddy, I'm sorry."

Gloria noted this exchange knowingly. She could see that she had her work cut out for her with this family for the next couple months. For now, she turned to Rod. Before she could speak, he had an answer for her.

"I refuse to say that I think Dad's an alcoholic on the grounds that it may incriminate me!" Rod tried to sound as if he were joking, but Gloria detected the underlying seriousness.

She looked at Mike directly. "Mike, so far you're the only one who says for sure that you're not an alcoholic. The other three wavered on the point. Let me ask you another question. Has alcohol caused problems in your life?"

Mike hesitated, then spoke abruptly. "A few."

"Okay," Gloria accepted this. "Nora, has Mike's drinking caused problems in your life?"

Nora looked at Jill and answered slowly, "Not so many."

Jill veritably exploded. "Aw, come off it! You guys make me crazy! You try to hide behind this big lie! Our whole lives are a lie! No problems? It's *normal* for Dad to get picked up on Main Street drunk?"

Rod leaned over and grabbed Jill's hand. "Come on,

Just as monarch butterflies are drawn to intense light, members of an alcoholic family network may concentrate their greatest energies on the intense people who cause the most intense problems within their families. Unfortunately, as they draw close—just as monarchs may singe their wings—family members often get burned.

Jillie, it's okay. Get ahold of yourself," he soothed.

Gloria watched Mike's face turn beet red and Nora's turn white. They were so shocked they were temporarily speechless. Jill sat back, looking amazed at her own display of emotions. She turned to Gloria, "I'm sorry. I think going through this divorce and all has made me overly sensitive to anything that has to do with alcoholism."

Gloria spoke to all four in an even tone. "I'd like to say this before we go on. Just as monarch butterflies are drawn to intense light, members of an alcoholic family network may concentrate their greatest energies on the people who cause the most intense problems within their families. Unfortunately, as they draw close—just as monarchs may singe their wings—family members often get burned.

"Of course, members of families who live with alcohol love each other just as any other family does. So they usually stretch and mold in any way they must in order to adapt and to try and make the tensions in their homes go away. A real problem, however, is that their homes are dysfunctional—that is, impaired in their functioning—and until an alcoholic family network gets help, the tensions *won't* go away. Jill is right to say that it is a real problem when someone gets picked up by the police for public intoxication—that's *not* 'normal.'"

"It doesn't mean I'm an alcoholic either!" Mike snorted.

Gloria replied, "I thought you said this isn't the first time you've experienced negative effects in your life because of alcohol."

Mike turned to Nora and looked at her meaningfully. Nora responded, "None we can't handle as a family, Gloria."

"I appreciate your assertiveness, Nora," Gloria said, "but I asked Mike the question."

The door to Mike's denial finally opened a small crack. "Okay! Okay! So, we've had a few problems because of my drinking. But I'm not going to drink anymore, so there won't be any problems."

This prompted Rod to comment, "Dad, c'mon, you know you haven't stopped drinking for more than a few weeks at a time since before Cole was born!"

"And just how do you know that, Mr. Smarty?"

"Because Mom told me," Rod answered.

"Oh?" Mike looked at Nora angrily. "Since when is this whole family against me? I get nailed for one little thing and just to get back at me you all gang together and give me this grief!"

"Us give *you* grief?!" Jill shouted. "What in the h—- do you call how you treat us?!"

Mike turned on Jill and looked at her scathingly. "How do I treat you, little girl?"

"Like a pile of dirt!" Jill spat back. "And I'm not a little girl—I'm a grown woman!"

"Hmpf," Mike sniffed. "Most grown women I know can take care of their marriages—you let yours go to the dogs like a baby would."

Jill's face crumpled. Mike had obviously hurt her deeply. Gloria suspected that Mike had used this same technique of ridicule in the past to bring members of his family "in line" and to control them according to his own needs. Now Jill was not to be stopped quickly. She bit back tears as she screeched, "Yeah! And wouldn't you know *I* had to marry someone just like good old Dad!"

Mike roared up out of his seat. Gloria thought he was going to hit Jill. Nora intervened by stretching an arm across Mike's waist and saying firmly, "Stop, now! You two settle down! We don't need to air our dirty laundry in front of Gloria."

Gloria looked squarely at Nora and said, "But, Nora, that may be precisely what you need to do."

The nervous tension caused by attending the counseling session, combined with the churning emotions that were just under the thin skin of this alcoholic family network, allowed some of the Martins' negative feelings to bubble out in this beginning therapy session. This encouraged Gloria a great deal. Some families had to come to counseling several times just to scratch the surface of their family's alcohol-related problems. But Gloria felt sure that at least a couple of the Martins were ready tonight to identify the truth of the family's illness.

Gloria turned to Rod. "How do you feel about what just happened?"

Rod's smile did not quite reach from his mouth to his eyes. "I don't know. I guess I'm used to it."

"This kind of thing happens quite often?" Gloria inquired.

"Well," Rod began to look like he felt trapped. "I mean, uhm, um, yeah, I guess—between Jill and Dad anyway."

"Your father and Jill don't get along—is that what you mean?"

"Kind of. They're a lot alike, so I suppose they butt heads more often than some."

"Do you have confrontations with your father, Rod?" Gloria asked.

"Sometimes, but I mostly just stay out of his way."

"I see," Gloria said. "Do you clash more often when he's drinking or just as much when he's sober?"

"When he's drinking," Rod muttered quickly.

"Pardon me?" Gloria wasn't going to let this opportunity slip away.

"I said when he's drinking," Rod stated matter-of-factly. He looked at his father.

Mike said, "You too, Rod? I can't believe this! I thought that of everyone you'd be the one to hang in there with me! I guess a man just can't depend on his family's loyalty anymore!"

Rod grimaced. "Dad, I'm not against you. I just have to be honest. Like Gloria said before, there's got to be some good reason Judge Harris sent us here."

Gloria looked at her watch. The session was more than half over. She let Rod's comment rest and said, "I'd like to explain a few things about the alcoholic family network."

Mike jumped right in. "Are you back to this alcoholic thing? Jeesh! Can't you give it a rest?"

"Mike," Gloria replied, "I'm not accusing you of being an alcoholic. Let's just say that I need to give you information about alcoholism to fulfill Judge Harris's orders. If you'll be so kind as to listen, from there on you can do what you want with the information."

Mike nodded and seemed satisfied with this. He relaxed a little. Nora breathed a loud sigh of relief at the change of mood. Jill still looked shaken, and Rod watched her with obvious concern.

"Okay," Gloria began, "I want to share some information about people who are at greatest risk of becoming alcoholic:

"One, males whose fathers suffered—or still suffer—extensively with alcoholism are highest on the list.

"Two, children of alcoholic parents or grandparents.

"Three, anyone who drinks often to get drunk, drinks more than five drinks at one occasion, or doesn't remember what happened after he or she drinks.

"Four, actually, *any* blood relative of an alcoholic is at high risk of becoming alcoholic."[1]

Gloria paused for a moment to gauge how receptive the Martins seemed.

Jill spoke as her eyes met Gloria's. "What is this information supposed to do for us?"

"Good question, Jill. I've told you these things in hopes that each of the four of you will honestly evaluate your risk of being or becoming alcoholic. I'd like you to share what was said at this session with Cole and Melanie so they can begin to assess their risk factors. If you decide, by our next session, that you're in the high-risk category, and that your drinking patterns indicate that you may already have a drinking problem, I'd like us to talk about that next week."

"Next week?" Jill seemed surprised. "Aren't you rushing us a little, Gloria? We don't even know if we can get Cole or Melanie to come with us."

"I can't really rush any of you, Jill. Whatever you need to deal with right now and what you're ready to handle will come out naturally as the opportunities arise."

Nora asked meekly, "Can you give us symptoms of a family that is definitely affected by alcoholism?"

"Certainly," Gloria answered. "Let me tell you some of the characteristics of an alcoholic's home life as seen from the perspective of his or her children or spouse:

"An alcoholic often makes promises to his loved ones, friends or others, and then breaks them.

"Within the alcoholic family network there is usually inconsistency and unpredictability. Rules change with the alcoholic's moods—sometimes he or she is loving and sometimes abusive.

"Feelings of shame and humiliation prevail in an alcoholic's home.

"Members of the alcoholic family network often feel unjustified guilt and responsibility for the alcoholic's drinking—commonly because the alcoholic blames his or her loved ones in subtle or blatant ways.

"Children in an alcoholic home may feel hurt, angry, abandoned and mistreated because the family's attention revolves around the alcoholic and how he or she is behaving at any given moment.

"Members of the alcoholic family network frequently feel lonely and isolated. They try so desperately to deny or hide the problems their family suffers that they don't even talk about it among themselves.

"Lying can actually become a way of life in the home affected by alcoholism, because family members may be trying constantly to cover up for the failings and unacceptable behavior of the alcoholic."² Gloria concluded matter-of-factly. "Does that help you, Nora?"

"Yes, thanks." Nora seemed to be digesting every word that Gloria had spoken.

"Do any of you identify with one or more of the facts about alcoholism in the family that I've listed?" Gloria looked at Mike closely. His hand was tapping up and down on the arm of the love seat. Nora looked at Mike too, out of the corner of her eye. Rod appeared to be thinking very hard.

Jill spoke. "Well, I certainly identify with just about everything you said!"

Mike glared at Jill but didn't speak. All of a sudden, he seemed to be extremely tired.

"Okay, Jill," Gloria prompted, "tell us one thing that stands out in your mind."

"Oh! That's easy!" Jill responded quickly. "The part about always trying to deny that there's a problem—just like we've done tonight!"

Now Mike snapped into action. "Jill, I'm warning you—if you don't stop trying to goad me and embarrass this family, I'll—"

"You'll what, Daddy?" Jill baited. "Beat on me like you do Mom?"

Nora's face turned ashen and she looked as though she might faint.

Rod turned on Jill in fury. "Jill! Stop this nonsense! I know you have some bones to pick with Dad, but leave Mom out of it! She's never done anything to you!"

"Oh, really?" Jill's voice dripped with sarcasm and pain. "And just how would you know, Rod? All you do is run away from the problems—just like everyone except me and Cole!"

"Cole!" Rod shouted in amazement. "Cole has his hands full with that alcoholic witch he married! When would he have time to work on *our* family problems?"

"For your information, Rod, Cole and I have both been to counseling on our own this past year!"

"A fat lot of good it did you!" Rod said bitterly.

Gloria intervened, "Excuse me, but time's up for this evening. We'll continue with this next week."

All four Martins looked at Gloria in disbelief. Mike spouted, "Thanks a lot! Get us all stirred up and at each other's throats and then send us packing! I'll be d——- if I'm coming back to this hornet's nest again—I'll do my time in jail!"

"I'm sorry you feel that way, Mike. I feel very good about the progress made this evening. You've opened up a wide range of feelings and issues to explore, and I think we'll make even more headway next week if you'll give it another try. I'll certainly recommend on my report to Judge Harris that this therapy be continued. I firmly believe it can be most beneficial to your family." Gloria stared Mike down.

Mike realized that this was something he must suffer through—the judge would never change his sentence now that this little snip of a counselor had gotten her claws into his family! D——-! If only he had called a taxi to drive him home that night! For now, Mike felt beaten and worn. He glanced back up at Gloria and said, "Well, we'll see."

"And you'll encourage Cole and Melanie to come also?" Gloria inquired.

"Yeah, yeah," Mike muttered.

"Good. Well then," Gloria said cheerily, "I'd like to thank you all for coming and for opening up. I can see that the next several weeks will be very interesting, and I think they could be extremely helpful to each of you! I'll look forward to seeing you next time."

The dismissal in her voice was all it took to make the Martin family rise. They walked slowly to the door and said quiet goodnights.

The Martins, each in his or her own way and time, needed to face the fact that their lives were affected by what Gloria knew to be alcoholism.

Mike denied being an alcoholic. But Gloria could see by what was said, the volatile emotions of the family and the different manipulations they used on each other that, in fact, Mike was at least a problem drinker. There were signs that he was (or had been) abusing his family mentally and emotionally, and Jill had indicated that Nora had been abused physically.

Jill was divorced from an alcoholic husband. She had stated that her paternal grandmother and one of Nora's grandfathers had been alcoholic. Rod said that their brother Cole was married to an alcoholic. And it was implied that Melanie Martin had a problem controlling her drinking.

All the elements were there. Gloria was glad to note that Jill and Cole had had some counseling on their own. Maybe they would be keys in helping the family break into the next stage of their recovery—examination.

She logged these notes in her report on the Martins' first counseling session. Then she closed up shop and went home.

Notes
1. Jane Brody, "Alcoholism All in the Family," (*Santa Barbara News-Press*, Santa Barbara, CA: 26 Aug. 1987).
2. Jane Brody, "Living Despite Alcoholism" (*Santa Barbara News-Press*, Santa Barbara, CA: 2 Sept. 1987).

Exercise One

Identifying problem areas in your life
Circle the appropriate number, with 1 as best and 4 as poorest.

Area One—General:

Right now, I feel:
1. Happy about the success I've achieved
2. Only a bit anxious and confused
3. Dissatisfied and frustrated
4. Miserable and out of control

Area Two—Self:
Using the categories above, circle the appropriate number following each question below.
1. Physical—How do you feel about your physical condition? **1 2 3 4**
2. Mental—What is your initial feeling when you think about the amount and kind of mental stimulation you have about you? **1 2 3 4**
3. Emotional—How do you feel about your emotional stability? **1 2 3 4**
4. Spiritual—When you think of your spiritual beliefs and values, how do you react? **1 2 3 4**

Area Three—Relationships:

1. With parents—What is your gut reaction when you think about your parents? **1 2 3 4**
2. With spouse—How do you feel when you look at your spouse across a room, or when you envision him/her when you're alone? **1 2 3 4**
3. With children—How do you feel when you hear your children coming out of their bedrooms in the morning or home from school in the afternoon? **1 2 3 4**
4. With friends—How do you react when you think of your closest friend? **1 2 3 4**
5. With employers (if you work for someone) or customers (if you are a business owner)—How do you feel when you think of those you depend on for your income? **1 2 3 4**
6. With neighbors—How do you react when you think of your neighbors? **1 2 3 4**

Area Four—Money and Career:

1. Job/business—How do you feel when you get up in the morning and consider going to your workplace? **1 2 3 4**
2. Possessions—How do you react when you look around your home, at your bank statements, automobile, or other material possessions? **1 2 3 4**
3. Work environment—How do you feel when you are in your office, store, factory, or other work area? **1 2 3 4**
4. Level of career/financial achievement—How do you feel when you think of where you are in life compared to your expectations when you first started out as an adult? **1 2 3 4**

Area Five—Physical Surroundings:

1. Area of the country in which you live—How do you feel when you think of your geographical location?
   1 2 3 4
2. Town where you're living—What is your reaction when you think of the community you live in? **1 2 3 4**
3. Your neighborhood—How do you feel when you drive or walk down the street of your neighborhood? **1 2 3 4**
4. Your home—How do you feel when you have special company coming for dinner and you survey your home just before they arrive?
   1 2 3 4
5. Your yard/patio/commons—How do you react when you look out your window at any outdoor space that's yours alone or that you share with other tenants? **1 2 3 4**

Evaluation

If you circled ones in nearly every area listed, you are denying that there's anything amiss in your life. If you circled nearly all fours, you are at the opposite extreme—doubting that there's anything good going on with you! Nobody's life is all bad or all good! However, there may be certain *areas* of your life that are shouting for special attention.

If you circled mostly ones or fours in a particular area, pay close attention to that part of your life. You may need to dig deeper to identify that, yes, you have problems in your relationships; and, yes, these may stem from being raised in a dysfunctional home.

Closely examine *any* area of your life that causes you to feel anxious, uncomfortable, depressed, hopeless, confused, frustrated or otherwise negative. These are the clues you need to honestly face the fact that there are problems in your life that may have roots in your background. Then you can begin to identify your problems more specifically. If you answered mostly twos and threes with a smattering of ones and fours, then you're likely a pretty healthy person with "normal" problems. Don't be afraid to delve into them, consider them and think of creative ways to solve them.

Problem-solving doesn't happen all at once. Rather, it often happens over a period of time. As you identify and confront problems, bear in mind that even negative feelings are *energy*. The key to your full recovery is to become aware of your problems, harness the energy, learn to use it to your advantage, and grow with it! Eventually, the negatives can turn into positives.

You probably know that there just aren't any cure-all answers for most meaty life issues. Realize that your age and phase of life make a difference in how you feel about things. Each decade of life brings unique demands and passages.

For instances, in our 20s we make the transition into adulthood. In their 30s many people are adjusting to marriage, parenting and career choices. In our 40s most of us have to accept issues surrounding middle age. During our 50s, we may have to confront an empty nest and the passing of our peak performance levels in several areas of life. In the 60s we must make the transition to being senior citizens. And in our 70s we face the fact that *we* are now the elderly of society.

Each of us attaches our own notions about any given age; but for the most part, each stage of life has its own rewards and disadvantages. Don't be overly concerned about minor troubles that may be due simply to the passage you are currently making. Do what you can to ease any tensions that exist and try to accept the things that are beyond your control right now.

Try to be patient with yourself and those around you. Even though you may be extremely excited about your progress and discoveries, hold back somewhat when discussing these with other family members who may not be as aware about the issues surrounding the alcoholic family network. Too much zeal may frighten your loved ones and close doors of communication.

Phil. 3:14 says, "I press on toward the goal to win the prize for which God has called me heavenward in Christ Jesus." Do the best that you can in living today and accept that that's sufficient. Press on!

Stage 2

EXAMINATION

Taking a hard look at the negative effects wrought in your life by living in an alcoholic family network.

The Impact of Alcoholism on the Family Network

During the week, Gloria pondered the Martin family's problems. The Martins had most likely come through a long string of crises over many years, and they seemed to be on the brink of finally letting an "outsider" into their tightly knit circle.

Before the Martins' second session, Gloria got a pamphlet from her files that described childhood experiences of a few individuals from alcoholic family networks. She would use it as a tool to help the Martins get beyond denial to accept the fact that alcoholism was involved in many of their traumatic experiences and dysfunctional relationships.

Gloria was pleased to see all six Martins show up for the second counseling session. Mike and Nora entered the office first. Then came Jill, Rod, and another young man Gloria assumed to be Cole.

Trailing slightly behind the rest was a girl Gloria would

never have guessed to be a part of this family if she happened to see them together in public. The other Martins dressed fairly conservatively and seemed quite conventional. This girl had extremely short, flame-red hair. Her skirt and jacket were made of a gauzy purple material that whipped around her as she flounced into the room. Combined with an orange blouse, dangling pink earrings and red boots, the girl's attired clashed angrily. Gloria suspected this to be an outer reflection of inner turmoil.

The girl turned to Gloria with a burst of energy and extended a hand. "Hi! I'm Melanie! I hear you caused some stir in this family last week. I thought I'd better come and at least check out the person who *dared* to cross Daddy!"

Gloria shook Melanie's hand and smiled openly. "Well, Melanie, it's nice to meet you. I don't recall 'crossing' your father, but I'm very glad you came along tonight."

Jill stepped forward and broke in quickly. "Gloria, Cole came along too. Cole, this is Gloria and vice versa."

Cole smiled shyly and shook Gloria's hand. He said, "Hello, I'm happy to meet you."

"Likewise, Cole! Thank you for coming this evening."

Everyone continued to stand. They seemed more nervous than they had been at the first session. Gloria took this as a sign that they'd each been making personal discoveries during the week and ought to be ready for the work she had for them.

"Please," Gloria smiled, "everyone take a seat. Tonight I have something for you to do that's a little different from last week."

"Aww," Melanie groaned, "I wanted to get in on baring our souls."

"Don't worry, Melanie, you'll have plenty of opportunity to say what's on your mind," Gloria assured her. "For now, however, I'd like you each to take a copy of this pamphlet and read it from beginning to end. It contains several interactions in different families struggling with problems caused by alcoholism. When you've finished reading, I'd like you to think about what the people experienced, how they felt and what you feel about their situations. Then you can examine how you've been affected."

Gloria handed out copies of the pamphlet and took notes as she observed individual reactions while the Martin family read. (See Appendix B for the pamphlet Gloria gave the Martins.)

One by one the Martin family finished reading. Gloria referred to her notes on each individual's reactions as they'd read. She wanted to discuss these and send the Martins home with plenty of personal issues to examine.

Melanie was the last to look up from the pamphlet. She looked agitated and teary-eyed. She swooshed the pages onto the coffee table in front of her and announced, "I have to have a cigarette! Do you mind?"

Gloria asked bluntly, "Do you need a cigarette to stop your emotions from coming out?"

"Whatever do you mean?" Melanie dodged.

"I mean," said Gloria, "that reading about other people's experiences—and possibly identifying with some of them—may have caused emotions to surface that you would rather stuff back inside of you by smoking a cigarette."

"Bull!" cried Melanie. "I am a very open and emotional person. If I feel something, I put it out on the table."

Jill grunted. Gloria turned to her. "Jill, did you have something to say to that?"

"Yeah." Jill straightened in her seat. "I'd like to ask Melanie how she could *not* be affected by the little girl who had an abortion. The same thing happened to *her* a few years ago!"

The sound that came from Melanie was like that of a raging animal. "How could you be such a traitor and bring that up? Here—in front of a stranger!"

Mike agreed loudly as he glared at Jill in disgust. "I should say so! What the h—- is wrong with you, Jill?"

Gloria intervened. "Jill, are you telling the truth? Did Melanie have an abortion a few years ago?"

"Yes, it's the truth," Jill said as she crossed her arms heavily across her chest.

"Melanie, is Jill telling the truth?" Gloria asked.

Melanie was visibly shaking as she nodded her head.

Gloria asked her gently, "Did the story about Tammy having an abortion affect you?"

"Um-hm." Melanie nodded again. Her arms were twisted around her as if she were giving herself a hug.

Gloria continued, "Can you tell me how you feel about it?"

Melanie's bottom lip quivered uncontrollably until waves of emotion cascaded out. "I feel like a *murderer.*"

Mike slammed a fist down on the coffee table and shouted at Gloria. "Now! See what you've done? Where do you get off causing people to feel like murderers? Who gives you the right to start fights in my family? You must be a pervert or something! You like seeing people in pain, don't you?"

Gloria responded in a normal tone. "No, I don't like to see people in pain. However, I know that people can often grow profoundly during some of the most painful times in their lives.

"Mike, I'd like to ask you why you accuse me of *making* Melanie feel like a murderer."

Mike sputtered in frustration, groping for words to justify his accusation. "Because . . . because you started all this! Just because!"

"Because isn't a workable answer, Mike. What 'all this' did I start?"

"My family into all this counseling crud!" Mike seemed momentarily satisfied with his answer.

"Did I force you to come to counseling?" Gloria asked.

"No!" Mike roared. "But you're sure making the most out of the chance the judge gave you to tear us apart!"

"Is that what you think I'm doing, Mike—tearing your family apart?"

"Of course! What else? Do you think it's making us *closer* to bring all this slime out in the open?"

"What slime, Mike?" Gloria inquired.

"These—these slimy feelings!" Mike hollered.

"Which slimy feelings, specifically?" Gloria prodded further.

"The ones where we end up calling each other names and telling secrets on each other!"

"Is it a secret that Melanie had an abortion?"

"Not now!" Mike huffed.

"Didn't you know about it before?" Gloria glanced from one member of the Martin family to another.

Melanie broke in. "They all knew about it. It just wasn't necessary for Jill to blab it to you."

"Does it bother you that I know, Melanie?" Gloria looked directly into Melanie's eyes.

Melanie responded frankly. "Not so much that you know. It's more the idea that I had one in the first place and that Jill would bring it up in front of others."

"Do you feel guilty about having an abortion, then?" Gloria wanted to know.

"Well, of course," Melanie answered. "Why do you think I feel like a murderer?"

Problems cannot be dealt with until you know what they are. Often, that does mean bringing them out into the open—even if it's painful to do so.

"You try to answer that," Gloria suggested. "Why do you feel like that?"

"Because I killed my baby!" Melanie moaned in exasperation.

"Did you think you were doing the right thing at the time?" Gloria asked.

"Sure," Melanie whispered. "I wouldn't do something like that unless I felt I had to."

"Are you saying that you did what you thought you had to do at the time, but now you regret your choice and feel guilty about it?"

"Yes!" Melanie wailed. "Yes! Yes! I feel guilty! Now what? You can't make my abortion go away!"

"No," Gloria said, "but I can suggest that you ask God to forgive you for what you did and that you follow His lead and forgive yourself. There just isn't anything you could do that God won't forgive you for if you'll go to Him and ask."

"Melanie?" Jill ventured softly, "can you forgive *me* for bringing this up? I didn't mean to hurt you—honestly I didn't."

"I know, Jillie," Melanie wiped at her eyes, "it'll be okay. I think we have to get this 'slime'—like Daddy calls it—in the open so we can scrub it away!"

"Very astute, Melanie!" Gloria said. "Problems cannot be dealt with until you know what they are. Often, that does mean bringing them out into the open—even if it's painful to do so."

Gloria turned to Mike. "Do you have anything you want to add at this point?"

"Hmpf!" Mike grunted. "It doesn't matter what I say—you're gonna do what you want anyway!"

"Did I force Melanie and Jill to bring their feelings out?" Gloria asked patiently.

"Guess not," was all Mike would say.

"Okay, then," Gloria glanced around the room. "We've covered some important ground this evening. If you will glance over the pamphlet again before next week's session, we can discuss how the stories sat with the rest of you and your different reactions to them. Remember, we want to examine if and how your family may be affected by alcoholism."

The Martins were particularly subdued as they left the room. Gloria's instincts and experience told her that at least part of the family was ready to begin confronting its problems.

Exercise Two

Examining the Problems by Day

Make a chart similar to the one below on each of seven sheets of paper or pages in a notebook. Label pages Day 1, Day 2 and so forth until you have a full week of days.

	What I Do:	How I Feel:
Wake-up Time		
Mornings		
Lunchtime		
Afternoons		
Dinnertime		
Evenings		
Bedtime		

Each day for one week, note in general terms what you do and how you feel in each of the time slots. For instance, if you work each morning, write "Work" in the

What I Do column. In the *How I Feel* column, write one to three words that describe how you feel at work. At the end of the week, look over these charts. Do you see any patterns? Are you usually depressed when you wake up? Is dinnertime particularly stressful for you? Is evening a time when you feel anxious?

Are any of your present feelings correlated to feelings from childhood? For example, perhaps evening was when your alcoholic parent was away from home drinking—or at home causing problems with the family. Perhaps you lay in bed and listened to your parents argue. If so, you may be uncomfortable around bedtime. Or maybe you worried about your parents at lunchtime on the playground at school. You may still get a knot in your stomach during your lunch break.

Do you have times each day which feel consistently good or bad? Try to determine root causes of your feelings.

What to Do

Build on the good times and minimize the bad. Reserve your most important duties and contacts for the good hours of the day. Try to take it easy or indulge yourself a little during the bad periods.

As you become more sensitive to problems by learning to read clues—such as feeling anxious, depressed or troubled during particular times of the day—you will become more nearly in tune with yourself and your specific problems.

Different People, Different Problems

As the Martin family's third counseling session drew near, Gloria turned her thoughts toward the family's problems. She looked over her notes from the previous session. There had been no real surprises to her trained counselor's eye. Mike had grown more and more sullen as he'd read the case studies of people from alcoholic family networks. Nora had turned pale and wiped at her eyes several times. Jill had curled into a ball while she read, as though she were trying to make a stomachache go away. Rod had read quickly and lain the pamphlet aside. Cole's face had taken on a tense, pained expression as he'd read. Melanie had wiggled in her chair and looked as though she were biting back tears through the entire ordeal.

Gloria had made deductions about how each family member was dealing with his or her problems, based on what Gloria considered to be a classic example of an alcoholic family network. But Gloria took care not to stereotype. She had observed, for example, that a child or spouse pinned with the label of "hero" often stayed in this role, or gravitated toward it. From an expert's point of view, Gloria considered the classic roles that family members played, but she also left plenty of room for their flexibility and growth.

Therefore, during the session that evening, Gloria planned to let the Martins talk back and forth to see how far along they might be in examining their own problems and feelings.

As Gloria was getting ready to get a cup of hot chocolate, there was a timid knock at her door. "Come in," Gloria said.

Melanie Martin stepped into the office. "Hi, Gloria," she said meekly. "I hope you don't mind that I came early."

"Actually, it works out fine tonight, Melanie. I'm glad to see you. I was just going to get myself some hot chocolate. Would you like some?"

"Sure, I need something warm—I'm shivering all over."

Gloria looked kindly at Melanie. She thought the shivering probably came more from rising emotions and nervousness than from being cold.

When the two women were seated with their chocolate, Melanie stared into her cup and then her eyes darted all around the room, avoiding Gloria's level gaze.

Gloria said softly, "Melanie, was there something you wanted to talk to me about?"

"Me?" Melanie nearly squeaked. "No, I just came early, that's all."

"I see," Gloria said, knowing better. "Where did you get such an interesting outfit, Melanie?"

"This old thing? Oh, I got it at a discount store here in town."

"Umm. You've worn a couple of unique styles here. Do you always dress so flamboyantly?"

Melanie looked down at her emerald green miniskirt, yellow leather boots, and lime-green sweater. She pulled at a large, yellow earring with one hand and the emerald green scarf at her neck with the other. She asked impishly, "Do you think this is flamboyant? Really? That's a nicer word for the way I dress than my parents use!" Melanie threw her head back and laughed. "Mom calls it gaudy, and Dad says it's just a bunch of horse pucky—if you know what I mean!"

"Yes, I know what you mean," Gloria nodded. "So you think your family looks at you as a joke?" she questioned. Melanie's response was a noncommittal shrug. Gloria changed the subject. "By the way, does your father use a lot of profanity, Melanie?"

"Not so much when he's sober." Melanie's direct reply was the lead-in for which Gloria had hoped.

"Do you mean that he does curse when he's drinking?"

"Uh, well," Melanie seemed to consider whether or not to back out. "Well, yeah, I guess he does."

"You seem cautious about answering that," Gloria stated.

"You bet I'm cautious!" Melanie wailed. "After last week I got a whole lot of crap!"

"Why?"

"H—-, I don't know! I'm always getting it!"

"Do you mean that you feel you are a scapegoat for your family?"

Melanie took a deep breath and let her shoulders drop hard as she exhaled. "I guess you're going to get me to talk anyway, so I might as well get to why I came early in the first place!"

"I'm glad." Gloria smiled, "but please tell me if you

think your family looks at you as a joke."

"Of course!" Melanie breathed. "I'm the one who dresses funny, talks funny, lives funny, and gives them all a way to unload their gripes!"

"What do you mean by 'their gripes'?"

"You know—all the crud that strangles our family— Daddy's drinking, Mom's putting up with him, Jill's divorce, Cole's unhappy marriage, Rod's being the middle man, and my wild life-style. If I can give them something to talk about by how I behave, then they don't spend so much time at each other's throats!"

"Do you think that's your responsibility, Melanie?"

"Well, *somebody's* gotta do it!" was the sure reply.

"Why does somebody have to do it?" Gloria asked.

"Ha! Because if somebody doesn't, we'd all probably rip each other to shreds and not have a family at all!"

"Let's pretend for a moment that you're right and the family does need someone to hold it together. Why you?"

"Because I'm the one who can take the heat!"

"Do you want to take this kind of responsibility, Melanie?" Gloria prodded gently. This was the right button— Melanie's emotional dam burst.

A couple of large, glistening tears coursed down Melanie's cheeks as she whispered, "No."

"Then why do you?"

"Because—I'm—" Melanie's chin quivered and the single tears turned into streams. "I'm the only one left."

"Left? What do you mean?" Gloria's heart went out to this girl in her suffering.

"Oh, I don't know!" Melanie cried. "Jill took it on for so long and it screwed up her marriage and she's nearly a basket case. Cole is so disappointed in his life and Rod can hardly face the fact that Daddy's an alcoholic at all. And Mom—"

Melanie's face twisted into such grief that Gloria went over to Melanie and put her arms around her. "What about your mom?"

"Sh-she's lived with so much already—I can't leave her to take it all on her own any more!"

"I'm a lot tougher than you think, Melanie." Nora's voice was steady. Gloria and Melanie turned to the doorway in surprise. Mike, Nora, Jill, Cole and Rod stood in a knot just outside the office.

Melanie quickly wiped at her eyes and said, "How— how long have you guys been standing there?"

"Long enough," Mike said purposefully. "I think it's time this family sat down and did some real talking."

In Mike's manner, Gloria recognized an alcoholic's acceptance that he had no choice but to deal with some of the turmoil in his family's life. She was ready for his desperate attempt to slip into the role of hero by "leading the pack."

The Martins grouped themselves around the coffee table. Nora sat close to Melanie and pulled her daughter's head onto her shoulder, stroking her hair as she had probably done when Melanie was little. Mike sat on the other side of Melanie. Jill sat with Cole on the love seat and Rod sat alone in a chair. Gloria surveyed them and braced herself for an emotion-packed 90 minutes.

Mike began. "Okay, kids, I want to say a couple of things." He cleared his throat. "In these last few months since I was picked up, went to court, and now to these sessions, I've been doing a lot of thinking. I've come to the conclusion that I do have a problem with drinking. After our first time here with Gloria, I thought I just wouldn't drink during the eight weeks of counseling to prove to myself and all of you that I wasn't an alcoholic. But I couldn't do it. I drank several times."

Every eye was glued to Mike. Everybody quivered with anxiety and uncertainty. Mike looked steady and sure. "I read those stories last week and thought at first that they were just self-pity trips people were on. Then through the week, little memories started coming back to me—things about while you kids were growing up. I couldn't remember all of your birthdays. I remembered Mom begging me to go to your football games, Cole, and me not wanting to because the guys were waiting for me at the pub. I thought about your wedding, Jillie, and how bombed I got and how I embarrassed all of you. I've been pretty hard on you, Jillie—"

"Daddy, stop!" Jill whimpered. "It's okay, Daddy, it's okay!"

"No, Jillie, it's not okay," Mike answered with a catch in his throat.

Gloria glanced around at the Martins. Jill looked as if she wanted to jump out of her skin. Cole was fighting back tears. Nora wept silently. Melanie looked absolutely astonished and Rod was sullen.

Mike swallowed hard and went on. "So many memories pop into my mind. So many things that I did—or didn't do. I started praying again—I haven't done that in years. I guess the 'Man upstairs' is helping me, because I never thought I'd be able to say how wrong I've been."

Mike's shoulders started heaving and great sobs began racking his body. "I'm sorry—I'm so sorry!"

In seconds, the other Martins surrounded Mike and were telling him, "It's okay."

Gloria let the family hug and cry for several minutes before she spoke. "Mike, you've just made a poignant admission and confession. I think that's wonderful! Many families never get to the point that you have tonight! Many adult children and spouses of alcoholics only dream that

You owe it to yourselves to get on with the business of examining the hurts and beginning the healing instead of trying to deny the damage.

they could break through the barriers as you have done for your family, Mike. That is a loving thing to do. I am curious, though, why the rest of you are saying that what Mike's done is okay, instead of acknowledging that he's right?"

Rod spun on Gloria. "Sheesh! Can't you give us a break? The guy just opens up his soul and you're right on our case!"

"Your father has just done a very courageous thing, Rod. I don't think it's fair to him if you pretend that all the years of suffering his alcoholism caused didn't exist. You owe it to him and to yourselves to get on with the business of examining the hurts and beginning the healing instead of trying to deny the damages."

"I'm with Gloria," Melanie piped up. "She's not out to hurt us, Rod. She's trying to help us!"

"How would you know, dingbat?" Rod asked acidly.

"Rod," Nora chided, "what's gotten into you?"

"I'm just sick and tired of all this!" Rod declared. "All my life I've been the one to try to keep peace on all sides. I've tried to be the 'good little soldier' so all this kind of junk wouldn't have to come up. Now we bring it up on purpose!"

Gloria took the opportunity to help Rod open up. "You know, Melanie thinks *she's* the one who's taken much of the burden of keeping things together by being different from the rest of you and channeling the attention of the family toward her. Are you saying you're the one who's taken the pressure, Rod?"

"Well, not in the same way Melanie says she has. As far as I'm concerned, Melanie just uses that as an excuse to be a dingbat and feel right about it."

"Do you think it's fair to call Melanie a name like 'dingbat'?" Gloria asked point-blank.

"I don't know!" Rod exclaimed. "What's the difference? She knows I don't mean anything by it."

"Do you know that, Melanie?" Gloria asked.

"No!" Melanie sat up straighter. "No! I don't know that! Everyone in this family calls me names like that and makes fun of me! And I'm tired of it! Rod, nobody asked you to be the little shepherd for all of us. Just because you're the baby in the family doesn't mean you're any great shakes compared to the rest of us!"

"Who said I was great shakes?" Rod stormed. "I just said that I've tried to keep the peace. I've watched all this poisonous stuff going on in our family all my life. I've tried to be the one who kept my head and didn't cause any waves. Now, we're making the waves on purpose!"

"Rod," Jill interjected, "who told you to be the guardian of the peace? There's no real peace in the way our family's been anyway. Take a look at us—we're *all* basket cases!"

"Jill," Nora spoke up. "I don't think that's a fair thing to say!"

"Mom? You of all people—" Jill snapped, "you're the biggest basket case of all! You're the one who put up with all the crap in the first place! If you had stood up for yourself none of this would've happened! You let Daddy drink, ridicule us, humiliate us, beat you and spend the family's money. You never did one thing to help us!"

"That's enough, Jill!" Cole roared. "You're not in a private counseling session now. Save your self-pity for your own shrink!"

Jill dissolved into tears. "Thanks a lot, Cole! You're a good support! At least I had the guts to ditch my alcoholic spouse! That's more than I can say for you!"

"Both of you *stop* it!" Mike bellowed. "Jill, you apologize to your mom!"

"No, I won't!" Jill nearly screamed. "She could've helped us kids and she didn't! Nobody did! Not Grandma, Grandpa, Aunt Jenny, Uncle Lowell, or anybody! Why? Why wouldn't anyone help us? They all knew what was going on!"

Nora's voice was barely audible. "Because everyone knew that what needed to be done was being done."

It was Melanie's turn to comfort her mother. "That's right, Mom, we know it. Jill's just upset, that's all. She doesn't mean it."

"Melanie," Gloria said, "do you think it's right for you to speak for Jill? She is telling how she really feels. It may be painful, but it is real and honest."

"Yes," Nora agreed. "She's being honest—and so will I. I could've left Mike. But I knew Mike couldn't help himself. I had four children to feed, clothe and shelter. I had no skills to earn enough money for all of us. And I loved Mike. If he'd gotten polio and been crippled I wouldn't have left him—and I didn't leave him because he has a problem with drinking, either. I did what I thought was best for all concerned. If that makes me wrong, then I guess I am."

"But, Mom," Jill pleaded, "why didn't you get help? Why didn't you make him stop? Why did you put up with his abuse? We grew up thinking we had to take every ounce of garbage that people threw in our faces because we believed that was the loving thing to do! I fell into my rotten marriage. Cole has his rotten marriage! There's not one of us that has diddly for self-esteem! Couldn't you see what you were doing?"

"Jill," Nora said in a stronger voice, "I never said that how I raised you was right. I never said that I don't have my own share of guilt to confess. I only said I did what I thought was best. I thought it was better for us all to stay together as a family and have faith that God would help us set things right one day—and I think that's exactly what He's doing now!"

Gloria heard a low wailing noise and turned to see Cole's shoulders heaving with great sobs. She asked carefully, "Can you tell me what's wrong, Cole?"

Cole looked up as if he'd forgotten anyone else was in the room. His eyes reflected inner pain and his voice rasped with torment. "I—uh—" he gulped for air. "Talking about Mom's letting all this happen just makes me nuts!"

"How so, Cole?" Gloria questioned.

Cole drew a deep breath in between his teeth. "Because!"

Gloria waited. She held up a hand when Nora tried to speak. Gloria kept her steady gaze on Cole. He opened up.

"Because—I couldn't make him stop hurting her! I was the oldest boy! I should've been able to help her! I should've been able to make him stop!"

"Are you referring to your dad?" Gloria asked tenderly.

Cole looked at her with eyes glazed in anguish and whispered, "Yes, I mean my dad."

Gloria watched Cole shake his head in guilty confusion. He still carried the weight of his childhood burden on his shoulders. Even as a man, he believed in his heart that he should have been able to help his mother.

No matter how irrational this feeling may seem to adults who know better, children who grew up with such intense feelings of responsibility often truly believe they have failed their loved ones. It would probably take Cole awhile to see that there was nothing he could have done to stop the abuse the family suffered because of Mike's alcoholism. Gloria knew it would do little good to try to convince him at this emotional moment that his feelings of guilt and shame were rooted in the abstract reasoning of a child. Hopefully, time would help him understand that his self-torture was unnecessary. For now, Gloria looked at Mike.

"How does all this make you feel?" Mike sat in the midst of his family looking totally helpless. He rubbed a hand through his hair and sighed, "I don't really know. Guilty, I guess. Scared. Sorry."

"Cole," Gloria changed directions abruptly. "You haven't said how you feel about Jill's bringing up your marital problems. Do you have anything you'd like to say about that?"

"Yeah!" Cole spouted, having regained some of his composure. This was a chance for him to save face in front of his family. "As a matter of fact, I do! First, I'm sick and tired of everyone talking about my rotten marriage to an alcoholic! Shel and I have had our full load of problems. But we're both going to counseling and Shel hasn't had a drink in more than a month—none of you even knew that, did you? And we're working it out as well as we can!

"Second, because of what we're going through as a couple, I can really understand what Mom's saying. We're all human and we do what we feel is best and try our hardest to make things come out all right! Third, I think it's important that we do bear in mind that Dad didn't become an alcoholic on purpose. It snuck up on him, just like Mom said about polio—a disease is a disease! And fourth, I think it's good that we're all able to be here doing what we're doing! There's no hope at all if things aren't brought out in the open—no matter how painful some of it is."

"Yea! Yea!" Melanie cheered. "Let's hear it for Cole!"

Her levity brought some much-needed relief from the

intense emotions. Gloria looked at her watch and said, "I think this is a good point to end on. We've opened up several different problems that alcoholism has brought into your lives. During the next two sessions, we'll be taking these and other troubles one by one and trying to recognize *why* you do some of the things you do. This week, be thinking about things in your own life that bother you and how these things may exist because of the alcoholism you grew up with. We'll be looking for patterns—past and present."

As the Martins settled down, Gloria thought it was a good time to recap and encourage them for the coming days. She knew that as thoughts, memories and emotions surfaced in each family member, there would be new wounds to heal. Old scars would be revealed, and there would probably be a few attempts to scurry back into the safety of old relationships. Even if those relationships were dysfunctional, they were all the family knew. It is human nature to feel safer with the familiar than with the unknown—even if what is known is pain and suffering.

"Each of you must remember that the key to your family's full recovery won't be found in a single hour, day, confession, or problem. It's going to be a process that will take many turns. The problems we have examined over the last couple of weeks have come out of some of your individual feelings, resentments, bitterness and anger. Next, we're going to get down to the work of isolating specific needs and areas to work on. Next week, bring a list of things that each of you, personally, would like help coping with.

"I wish we could address all the issues in one session, but there are just too many! I want to get to your drinking, Mike, so that we can help you to stop. We'll talk about other support groups for you and ways that your family can help you. But we have to take one session at a time, one week at a time; in between, I'd like to leave you with a Bible verse.

"In John 14:14 Jesus says, 'You may ask me for anything in my name, and I will do it.' I will be asking God for your healing, strength and comfort. Pray for guidance and whatever else is on your mind—you *will* be heard!

"Just hang on! You're not alone, and things will be happening to help you each get on a healthy track. You must be patient, and let time take its course. You may even have dreams in which your true feelings about each other and your life come out."

As the Martins left that evening, Gloria uttered a silent prayer of thanksgiving to God for His help and love. Without Him, there would be no hope for the hundreds of thousands like the Martins, riddled with the problems and pressures of an alcoholic family network.

Exercise Three

Examining the Problems by Night

Keep paper and a pen by your bed. As soon as you wake up each morning this week, write down what you've dreamed. If you can't remember dreaming, then write that down. Date each day's entry. Compare what you've dreamed at night to what was going on in the daytime as you read over your daily charts from the previous exercise. Were there challenges or events during the day which you dreamed about that night? Are there ongoing concerns that you're dreaming about frequently? Your dream life may hold clues about problems that are nagging you or holding you away from inner joy.

What to Do

Try to relax completely as you get into bed at night. Let your mind and body go totally limp. Imagine yourself lying in a lush, green meadow with the sun warming you and a gentle breeze wafting over you. Ask in prayer that you will dream about any problems you aren't consciously aware of. Pray that you'll be able to remember your dreams and think through them during the day.

If you are unable to remember your current dreams,

consider any past dreams that stand out in your mind. Certain types of dreams are quite common for members of the alcoholic family network. You may already have experienced:

1. Dreams in which you save your family from disasters such as fires, floods, robbers or tornadoes
2. Dreams in which you are trapped in a place or circumstances from which you can't seem to escape
3. "Worry" dreams, in which you can't get to a loved one who needs help
4. Dreams in which you want or try to be someone else
5. Dreams in which you are "pushed" into doing something or being someone with whom you're not comfortable
6. Dreams in which you chastise others (or are chastised yourself) for not taking life seriously enough or, conversely, for taking life too seriously
7. Dreams of animals that stalk small prey. One night you may dream that you are being stalked and the next night that you are doing the stalking.

One adult child of an alcoholic used to dream frequently about an organ grinder who had a monkey on a leash. After several months, it occurred to her that this dream symbolized how she felt about her life—the organ grinder was her alcoholic mother, and she was the monkey required to perform at the organ grinder's command.

Sift through your past and present dreams for symbolism and patterns. Are there recurring nightmares? Are there "wish" dreams in which you do or say things that you don't dare to say or do openly or consciously—such as tell an alcoholic parent or spouse exactly what you think of him or her?

Pay close attention to how you feel as you wake up. Do you dread meeting the demands of another day? Do you wake up with a tense jaw, already anxious about what the day is going to bring? Do you awake with a sense of pessimism and gloom?

Let the things that turn up in your dream notes simmer in your mind for several days or weeks. Put them on the back burner and one day understanding may dawn about a particular problem. Sometimes the subconscious will work out things that we don't know about or can't face consciously.

Don't be frightened by your dreams. Some children and spouses of alcoholics are terrified by dreams in which they try to kill an abusive parent or spouse. Remember that dreams are symbolic—not real! Meet them head-on and they may produce just the clues you need to solve some of the problems that riddle your life!

You needn't feel guilty about your dreams. Remember that, even if you can't share them with anyone else, God knows them already and understands you completely! First John 3:20 says, "For God is greater than our hearts, and he knows everything."

One of these nights you may just dream a new dream for yourself—one that will help you become the healthy, loving person God wants you to be!

Stage 3

RECOGNITION

Realizing why you act, react, feel, think and interpret
things the way you do.

Why Am I This Way?

The Martin family arrived promptly for their fourth session. This made Gloria very happy, because it was common for people at this stage to try to avoid further emotional upheaval by backing out of counseling. Of course, backing out provides only temporary relief—forcing the raw energy of emotions into less desirable channels.

Gloria began the session by telling the Martin family that, unless the alcoholic family network confronts their problems head-on, negative emotions release themselves in other ways:

1. unhappiness in the work place
2. lack of self-motivation to change
3. physical ailments
4. mental depression
5. anxieties or phobias
6. loneliness
7. self-pity

8. hostility
9. feelings of being out of control
10. repeating unhealthy patterns of behavior—
    especially in relating to others
11. fear of authority figures
12. lack of self-discipline to follow projects through
    from start to finish
13. difficulty enjoying good times
14. loyalty to people or circumstances that may be
    destructive
15. incessant feelings of being the "odd man out"
16. over-exaggerating (lying about) things
    unnecessarily
17. exhibiting an insatiable need for approval from
    others
18. being overly critical of self
19. feeling responsible for the well-being of others
    (sometimes to the exclusion of self)
20. becoming addicted to excitement and crisis.

The Martins listened intently as Gloria named some of
the more prominent problems displayed within the alcoholic family network. She told them, "People in families
affected by alcoholism are like the roots of willow trees—
they grow in whatever direction is necessary to reach
water for their survival. Each member of the alcoholic
family does whatever he or she has to do to reach the
"water" he or she needs to get by. The trouble is that, like
roots that may grow through a sewer line or bump up
under a sidewalk, members of an alcoholic family network
usually have to deal with many undesirable consequences
of their well-intentioned efforts to get along in life."

Melanie commented with a laugh, "I remember when
we were little I could always find Cole under the willow

tree in our front yard if he wasn't anywhere else! Maybe he was checking for roots!" Dressed in a black suit with fuschia blouse, jewelry and heels, Melanie seemed to have less need tonight to create a shock effect.

Cole smiled. "No, Melanie, I went there when I was scared or mad or otherwise bummed out."

Gloria asked, "Why the willow tree, Cole?"

"Because it seemed so safe under there. The long branches draped all around and hid me from the rest of the world. Inside was a whole, private place—little things like bugs and worms lived there." Cole grinned. "I used to have pet ladybugs. The red ones were Mrs. Apples and the green ones were also Mrs. Apples."

"Hey!" Jill exclaimed. "My safe place used to be under the porch, sitting in the crawl space. Wish I would've thought of the willow tree, though—it was probably a lot cleaner!"

Gloria said, "You know, even as adults we need a willow tree—or a crawl space. We each need to have a place we can go that's all our own, where we don't feel threatened. A spot where we can really let down and be by ourselves. That place may be a physical place, but it can also be a mental break—a time we take just to pause and unwind with our own company. For myself, I like to take a long walk in the evening and think things through—especially if I'm disturbed about something. Some people take hot baths, garden, bike or otherwise regroup and release their emotions."

Rod quipped, "You mean 'normal' people have to have hiding places too?"

"Ah," Gloria nodded, "I'm glad that came up. You know, one of the things that can hold back alcoholic family network members from full recovery is the huge brick wall around them that keeps them guessing at what normal is.

They may sense that their family isn't healthy, but they don't know for sure what *is* healthy. Sometimes members of an alcoholic or otherwise dysfunctional family try to imitate television families, thinking that these portray what healthy families are like. But there is no two- or three-hour-long show that could ever reveal what a healthy family is like.

"Families change constantly. Their feelings, moods, interactions and behavior are never the same for two days in a row. Alcoholic families argue, get depressed, laugh, celebrate, cry and grow weary, just like healthy families.

"I had a client who thought that healthy families didn't fight or show frustration. He stuffed any anger or hostility he felt inside himself and refused to express it because he didn't know there were healthy ways to do that. He married a woman from a well-adjusted family. At a dinner with his in-laws shortly after their wedding, his bride abruptly told her sister to shut up and not interrupt when her husband was talking to their dad. The husband was quick to say that it was okay. But his new wife exclaimed that it was *not* okay and her sister should apologize. The sisters exchanged a brief flurry of angry words. My client told me it made his stomach knot to hear them arguing—especially because he thought he had caused it!

"In reality, this young man did not *cause* the sisters' reactions. And the fact that the girls expressed negative emotions did not mean that there was anything wrong with them or that they did not love each other.

"Negative emotions can seem like a real threat to someone who has grown up in an alcoholic family network. Expression of negative emotions seems necessary to avoid at all costs. Members may think that if they get too angry at or inconsiderate of someone, that person may stop caring for them or even stop being their friend. This

You've all learned how to act when Mike is drinking—but not how to deal with him or your places in the family when he's sober. You have to learn new ways to interact with one another as you all get healthier.

is absolutely untrue in sincere relationships.

"In sincere, healthy relationships, people are free to express themselves—without being abusive. However, no family is *completely* free of problems or its own neuroses! Most healthy people have unhealthy quirks in their personalities and relationships. We are all human—we will have negative, uncomfortable feelings to cope with. The key is finding ways to get these feelings out of our systems without destroying others or ourselves. Ephesians 4:31 says, 'Get rid of all bitterness, rage and anger, brawling and slander, along with every form of malice.' It says to 'get rid' of it, not hold it inside. There's a very good reason for that. Negative feelings that are held inside are like cancer that spreads to every part of our lives. In one way or another—maybe in ways I mentioned earlier—the poison will come out.

"That's why it's important to find harmless avenues to get rid of the sludge in our hearts. These may include physical exercise, telling someone plainly how you feel about something he or she has done to you, prayer, writing, painting, singing, playing a musical instrument, and reading good books that help teach the life skills you need to recover fully from your alcoholic background.

"*'Healthy' is whatever feels good, works right, and is uplifting for most of the family members most of the time.* There will be plenty of occasions in a normal family when not everyone is happy at the same time. But knowing that everyone accepts and cares about you regardless of what you're feeling provides a wonderful, loving environment where you can be secure and nurture yourself."

"Gloria," Nora interjected, "I don't mean to change the subject, but something you said reminded me—I have something to show you."

"That's fine, Nora. We'll be addressing all of the things

I've been talking about throughout the rest of our counseling sessions. What did you want to show me?"

"Well, the first time we were here, I believe Jill brought up the fact that my grandfather was an alcoholic. I never really knew that for sure. But this last week I started reading my Bible again after a long period away from it. In the Bible I found a news clipping that I thought the rest of the family should know about—it may help us to see that alcoholism *is* a disease and that a tendency toward it can be inherited."

Nora handed Gloria a yellowed piece of paper. Gloria read it through. "Your grandfather?" she inquired.

Nora nodded.

"Well, this certainly would indicate that there is something to Jill's comment."

"What?" Jill asked anxiously. "What does it say?"

"It says that your great-grandfather was found in an alley early one morning, dead from exposure. It says that there didn't appear to be any foul play because his wallet, money, and pocket watch were untouched. An empty fifth of whiskey was in his hand," Gloria responded.

"That doesn't mean he was an alcoholic," Rod said.

"No, it certainly doesn't," Gloria acknowledged. "But a person would have to assume that someone dying from exposure with a fifth of whiskey in him was either too drunk to take care of himself or was purposely trying to harm himself. Either choice would indicate a serious problem that was related to alcohol—at least at the time of death."

"Well," Nora explained, "after I read that I started remembering little bits and pieces of conversation from when I was a girl. I seem to recall that whenever my grandfather was mentioned someone would either hush up right away or call him an old lush."

Gloria nodded, "Very likely. Years ago, little was known about alcoholism. In fact, there wasn't much recognition of, sympathy or treatment for the disease at all. It's only been in the last decade that people have been able to begin to admit to, confront and cope with the problem openly, allowing much more research and help to be made available. Now, members of families like yours can call on several nationwide support groups for help in solving many of the problems we've brought up and will talk about in more detail.

"For instance, I'd like to suggest that you begin going to Alcoholics Anonymous (AA), Mike. I know there's a meeting once a week in your town. Nora, you may like to go to weekly Al-Anon family group meetings—these are for family members of alcoholics. If you had teenagers I'd suggest Alateen for them. As for the rest of you, I'd be thrilled if you would come here, to my building, every Thursday night for meetings with the Adult Children of Alcoholics group."

"There's no way I'm going to AA," Mike stated. "I'd feel like such a loser getting up in front of people and telling them that I have a problem with drinking!"

"I know that's how a lot of alcoholics feel, Mike," Gloria said compassionately. "But you know, being surrounded with people who truly understand and identify with you can be a tremendous support, and you'll need it to stop drinking and live sober. If you can't bring yourself to go right now, then keep it in mind for a time when you may feel you do need it. As you work through your problems, your family members will be working through their own. They may not have very much emotional strength left over to help you get sober because their own needs will demand that they nurture themselves. Going to a support group can provide the bridge of understanding and acceptance that people need to cross over from unhealthy lives to full recovery."

Nora wanted to know, "What are some ways we can help Mike and each other?"

Gloria smiled warmly at Nora. What a gentle, caring woman she seemed. "Well, the first way I want to talk about is to put God at the center of your lives."

Rod snorted, "You know, Gloria, God is fine for regular people, but He's not for me."

"Why not, Rod?"

"I don't know. I guess I just figure He's for the guy who takes the time to go to church every Sunday and who doesn't have a family life like we do."

"You know, Rod," Gloria answered, "many members of the alcoholic family network go through periods—or their whole lives—feeling like the exceptions to every rule, good or bad. Another common, deeply rooted feeling is that you're the one exception to God's ability to completely love and help—meaning you're the one He can't love and help."

"I've felt like that before," Jill piped up. "I've wondered if God could ever forgive some of the anger and hate I've had toward Daddy and Mom."

Gloria replied quickly. "God knows every negative, hateful thought any of us has ever had and He can still love, forgive and help us! God knows about every time you may have wished your drinking parent would disappear from your life. God knows if you daydreamed that a wonderful new partner came into your non-drinking parent's life and made things 'all right' for the whole family. He knows every time you may have lied just to say the right things to ward off a verbal or physical attack by your alcoholic parent. God knows each and every tear of fear, anger, bitterness, frustration and despair that you've ever cried. He loves you with the same amount of grace, mercy, care and salvation as He loves His other children—including your alcoholic parents!

"Tonight I wanted you to examine further why you react and feel the way you do about things that have their roots in your alcoholic family network. Please take out the lists I asked you to bring to this week's session. Let's see if we can find some ways for you to help each other."

Gloria noted thankfully that every member of the Martin family had brought a list of his or her own problems. She knew that examining oneself and being able to identify the negatives was a big, healthy step toward full recovery.

Gloria said, "I'd like you each to tell me about a particular problem and why you think it exists in your life. Rod, you're the youngest. Do you want to go *first*, for once?"

"Thanks a lot. You're a real pal to let me be the leader on this one," Rod grinned. "But I will. I only have three things that are really bothering me right now. First, I don't really like us poking around in our feelings at these counseling sessions. Second, I can't seem to relate to a lot of what my brother and sisters are saying. Third, I don't think Dad's really harmed anyone and we're being unfair to him. As far as why I think these are problems for me right now, I think it's obvious—I don't want to deal with them! It's easier just to let them go!"

"Very insightful!" Gloria exclaimed. "I would agree that your reasoning is right on target! The fact that you can say it out loud is a very good thing. Let's keep in mind that this is the way you feel, and next week, one of the first issues we'll address is why it may seem easier just to let things go and not deal with them. Melanie, you're next."

Melanie cleared her throat. "I guess mine are a little more self-centered. I'm concerned with why I can't seem to get a promotion at work; why I always seem to end up dating guys that want to take advantage of me; why I always want to shock people, and why I'm so defensive when anyone tries to tell me how to do something. The reasons why these are problems? Who knows! It's anyone's guess!"

Gloria made some notes on her paper. "Okay, Melanie, next week we'll talk about why you find yourself in the middle of these types of things. Cole, do you have your problems ready?"

"Yeah," Cole nodded grudgingly. "I'm really not all that thrilled with opening myself up to this in front of everyone else in the family, though."

"Cole," Gloria said, "I think that indicates you've been honest with yourself about the problems you listed— otherwise you wouldn't feel you were taking a risk. When it comes to honesty and working on problems, taking risks is definitely worth it!"

"Okay. Well, I wrote that it's a problem for me that my family's always putting Shel down. We've been married for three years now and they just won't accept her!"

"That's not true!" Nora interrupted.

"Nora," Gloria chided, "let's let Cole's problems be his own. Whatever he feels *is* valid. Next week we'll discuss how each of you feels about what everyone else says tonight, after you've all had a chance to think through what the others say."

Cole went on. "I'm also bothered by the fact that I married an alcoholic and now I'm tied to loving her the rest of my life. But that leads to my next problem—guilt! I even feel guilty for feeling trapped! Now, when Shel is getting help and she's been sober, I still have this feeling like, 'So what? Nothing good's going to last anyway— everything falls apart eventually.'"

"That's very articulate, Cole. You seem to have a good handle on what's bothering you. Can you give me your version of why these are problems?"

"Um, I think it's pretty obvious—growing up in a family with alcoholism," Cole answered.

"Maybe that's the umbrella your problems come under, but I think it's simplistic to use that and not look deeper into it. We'll examine other possible reasons next week. Jill?"

Jill looked at Gloria and said, "I—uh—I don't want to tell mine tonight!"

"Why?"

"Oh! Just because!" Jill was very agitated.

"Jill," Gloria began gently, "it's okay if you don't tell your list of problems tonight. Just keep them with you for next week and maybe you'll feel like sharing them. Nora, will you be next?"

"Yes," Nora obliged. "I have three things on my list. First, it seems like I'm always tired and trying to catch up with things. I think it's because I'm forever taking on too many things to do at one time. I guess life just happened to me and I got tired out. Second, I sometimes suspect that I'm living at a low-grade level of depression all the time. Maybe this is because, again, I got so busy living and surviving with the family that I never really chose anything for only me to get involved in."

Nora hesitated several seconds before she continued. "I don't know that I really want to say this last one, but I do want to be honest and set an example for the kids, so I will. Since we started counseling I've found myself—" she stopped.

"Go ahead, Nora," Gloria urged.

"I—" Nora held her list in both hands and stared down at it. Gloria saw a tear fall but remained silent. In a moment Nora raised her head. Her cheeks were wet with tears. She almost whispered, "I resent Mike for causing this family *more* fuss and heartache." She gulped and rushed on, "Not because I don't want him to get better—I do want him to be sober—but I don't know how to act. I resent that he's causing all this stir and I have to pay even more consequences because of him—it was bad enough to raise these kids under tough conditions—now I have to put up with this counseling and I feel so—so humiliated that someone outside our family knows so many private things about us!"

Gloria let Nora catch her breath before speaking. "That was very brave. I think you have shown your family an admirable example of the recognition process, Nora. Next week we'll look in depth at the reasons for your feelings. For your peace of mind, however, I do want to add that your feelings of resentment and confusion over how you feel about Mike are very normal and quite common for non-alcoholic spouses—and even the children of the alcoholic family network. You've all learned how to act when Mike is drinking—but not how to deal with him or your places in the family when he's sober. You have to learn new ways to interact with one another as you all get healthier.

"Mike, would you talk now?"

Mike balked. "I don't know. I feel so bad after listening to Nora, it doesn't seem right that I have any problems."

"Mike, if you didn't have problems before you became an alcoholic, the disease has to have created some. Your feelings are just as valid as Nora's."

"Okay. Well, my list is just of single problems: guilt, shame, too much pride, bitterness, feeling like a failure and terrible loneliness! No one really understands me. You know, I wouldn't have drunk in the first place if I wouldn't have had so many pressures and nobody to listen except my friends. I mean, a guy goes to work every day, and comes home to crying kids, a tired wife, more bills to pay and stuff to do around the house! The only place to get away from it is down at the pub with my buddies—they understand me! I think I deserve to get away from it all once in a while!" Mike sighed. "I guess my life is kind of a mess. Now I suppose you're going to tell me that too much booze caused all these problems!"

"At this point, Mike, you are sorting through so many things that we may need to let them fall under the general category of alcoholism. Later, we'll isolate specific problems. I do want to point out, though, that alcoholism isn't necessarily drinking too *much* booze—it's any kind of *dependency* on alcohol. We'll talk more about your feelings next week, too. For now, I think we've had a very big night," Gloria said.

The Martins looked drained, but more relaxed than they had at the end of other sessions. This gave Gloria a good indication that real headway was being made in the recovery process.

She finished up the evening with encouragement. "You are all doing so well! Just keep letting one day follow the next—you will continue to recognize areas of your lives that need work *and* areas in which your lives are improving!

"During this week, think about your own behaviors, feelings and problems. But also think about those of your other family members. By considering their problems and feelings, you are taking the biggest leap toward being able to understand and help one another. Encourage one another to open up honestly, and try not to ridicule or deny the others' emotions."

Exercise Four

Mapping Your Reaction Patterns: People

On a sheet of paper, make a chart like the one on the next page, leaving plenty of room to write. Finish the statement for each of the people you list. Be honest.

Look closely at those negative feelings. If you can't think of any, look again. It is a very rare—and almost superhuman—individual who doesn't have negative feelings toward someone in his or her life at any given moment. Don't be ashamed of negative feelings—remember that these feelings are an energy force; the shame is when the negative feelings are left to fester and burst later in our lives with unnecessary physical, emotional, mental or spiritual poison!

It is much healthier to identify the negative feelings so that we can begin to understand why we feel, behave and believe the way we do. Through understanding, we can gain knowledge and wisdom about ourselves. Once we learn to honestly examine our problems and recognize where they come from, we can begin to loosen the unhealthy grip they have on our lives.

There are many things that we do or say without giving thought to what *really* bothers us and why. Many negative feelings may be senseless leftovers from our past—

I feel resentment, anger, envy, guilt, hatred, irritation, or mistrust toward:

Who: Why: How it shows:

My Parents

My Spouse

My In-laws

My Boss

My Children

My Friends

My Pastor

My Neighbors

Myself*

Other:

Other:

Other:

and we eat them day after day until they eat us! For instance, you may still resent your parents for not allowing you to attend a dance during high school—and not even realize it. You may mistrust your boss and come to understand it's because she reminds you of your alcoholic mother or wife.

You may be irritated with your in-laws because you

---

*You may be surprised to discover that you turn many negative feelings toward yourself so you don't have to face your anger toward anyone else.

think they are trying to run your life, but in reality, you are insecure and threatened by their harmless advice or suggestions. You may envy your neighbor and realize it's because you hear the merriment of her well-adjusted family enjoying each other's company in her home. You see the with resentment because your family can't get together in fellowship like that.

You may not be aware that you show your negative feelings toward others by ignoring, criticizing, laughing at or chastising them. But your growing awareness of the who, why and how of your negative feelings can free you to grow, change and become a stronger and more joy-filled person.

What to Do

Sit down and look over your completed chart. Have a stern talk with yourself about the negative feelings you may be harboring toward others. Ask yourself the following questions and give yourself the gift of honest answers:

1. Are there patterns in the list of people for whom I have negative feelings? (E.g., Are they mostly people I see as authority figures? Are they "outsiders"—under no obligation to be involved with my family problems—whom I resent for not solving my problems? Are they individuals whom I've idealized as not having problems of their own and therefore I resent or envy them because of their joy?)

2. Are there negative feelings that I need to simply let go of? (E.g., Anger over inconsiderate remarks which the speaker may not have intended; hatred for any real or imagined slights; bitterness over someone else's happiness or triumphs to which I felt entitled.)

3. Are there negative reactions I have displayed

toward others for which I need to make amends? (E.g., Do I need to apologize to a friend for turning my back when she was awarded for an accomplishment? Do I need to explain to my neighbor that I want to be glad that her family is well adjusted, but I'm sad that my own family can't enjoy getting together? Should I tell my mother I'm sorry I blamed her for my not fitting in with the peer group of my choice in high school?)

4. Are there negative feelings that I need to admit to in order for them to begin dissolving? (E.g., Do I tend to hold back affection for loved ones because I resent them for [supposedly] not loving me enough? Am I jealous of my spouse's achievements? Do I harbor feelings of hostility toward my children simply because I am not always happy to be a parent?)

5. Is my life truly miserable because of others—or because I refuse to take responsibility for my own happiness? (E.g., Am I tolerating the abuse of an alcoholic spouse because I think it's the right thing to do, or am I scared out of my mind that if I don't, he or she will leave me all alone? Am I resigned to a life of poverty because I think it's my "destiny," or because I refuse to make the effort to get more education, to get a better career, or generally to learn how to make a more profitable way for myself? Am I blocking paths for my personal or marital growth out of spite against an alcoholic parent—trying to "show him/her" the damage they've caused?)

6. Is there one real, healthy advantage for hanging onto negative feelings? (E.g., Is my life going to be better if I refuse to swallow my pride and make amends with my sister? Am I ever going to achieve real fulfillment if I stay in a dead-end job? Will I become the person God wants me to be if I stay stuffed with emotional poison?)

7. Is thinking of change really as scary as thinking of

living out my life filled with anger, hatred, resentment, envy and other negative feelings? Is it worth digging into why I feel, behave and believe the way I do in order to find a better, more peaceful way to live? Am I prepared to shed some tears, experience some headaches and other temporary anguish in exchange for a new, happy and powerful way of life? Does it make sense to ignore negative feelings and pretend they aren't clues to problems within myself?

Ponder these questions, even if you can't answer them right now. Things may come to light over a period of days, weeks or months that cause you to say, "Ah-ha! *That's* where that jealousy comes from!" or, "*Now* I see why I'm so envious of their marriage!" Just as kicking into dusty pebbles at the side of the road can turn up a shiny quarter, your mental probing can turn up realizations that will help make your life "shinier"!

Remember that understanding *why* you are who you are can help motivate you to learn *how* to change the negative energy in your life into a positive force!

Sorting Through the Rubble

Gloria studied her notes on the Martin family's last session. She knew that for an alcoholic family network, or any one member of it, to truly recover from their wounds and heartbreaks, the power of God was necessary. She also knew that recognition of problems was a prerequisite to getting wisdom and understanding about them. She prayed silently that the Lord would build a hedge of protection and love around the Martins as they tried to overcome the effects of alcoholism in their lives.

All six members of the family showed up promptly. Gloria started the session with a warning against self-pity. "As we discuss your individual problems and their origins, try not to get mired in thinking, 'My childhood is responsible for all my struggles! That's why I'm witchy, a liar, defensive, phobic or depressed.' Remember that *all* parents, including those who maintain a healthy, happy home, have their own weaknesses and faults. Kids from so-called healthy homes can also grow up emotionally crippled in one area or another. A very shy child may just happen to be born to a pair of extremely outgoing parents. Though this couple may be healthy and loving, their child might grow up under great pressure to act like someone she's not.

"Of course, most parents do not intend to hurt or scar their children. But, after all, parents don't come to their positions with Ph.D.s—they come by way of observing others. And this observation is from the perspective of a growing child—not a mature adult. A mother may seem to be constantly irritable. But her irritation might stem from being forced to spend her time being concerned over where next week's grocery money is coming from; she may not have enough energy left over to do lots of fun things with her kids. A father may not be able to express his love to his children in words. Perhaps he didn't have anyone who expressed love to him either; he may need help learning how to be affectionate.

"As you can imagine, the potential number of situations in which parents can damage their children's self-esteem is countless. Regardless of the circumstances in which you grew up or lived, there is a point you must reach in order to become a truly whole person—a point where you can say, 'Too bad if I am emotionally crippled because my parents were alcoholic, broke, physically abusive, criminal, or just regular people doing the best they knew how! I will be on this earth for one lifetime and I must take responsibility for the quality of my life while I'm here. I needn't be miserable or make those around me miserable because of my childhood or present problems! I must face my own problems and weaknesses. I must recognize why I have them and then push myself on toward reconciliation and the full recovery of my personality!'

"During the stages of identification, examination and

recognition, you face the problems in your life, analyze them and find their origins. The next stage, reconciliation, can help you break the barriers between plain existence and real living. Restoration can be an exhilarating and rewarding process of finding God's plan for your life, as I talked about last week, and discovering your 'whole' personality. The recovery process can then come full circle to completion. However, no healthy, well-adjusted person ever stops growing, changing, stretching, thinking, feeling or challenging him or herself!

"Tonight I want to go more deeply into the things that you each said were bothering you last week. Rod, you went first. Do you have anything to add before we start?"

"Nope. Full steam ahead!"

"All right," Gloria said, "then let's begin. Rod, you said that you really don't want to deal with all this and wondered why it seemed easier just to let it go. Am I right?"

"Uh-huh," Rod acknowledged.

"Okay. Can you tell me what part of this bothers you the most?"

Rod sat up straighter in his chair. "I guess I feel that however any of us may feel about each other, it's better just to keep it to ourselves most of the time. I mean, nothing we can say now will change what's done! I don't think Dad meant to hurt any of us and I don't think it's fair to grind all of our faces into the mud just so we can get it off our chests!"

"Those are valid feelings, Rod. I'm hearing you say that you see counseling as an excuse to throw accusations and insults at your dad. Is that right?"

"Kind of. Yeah! That *is* right. I feel like this is a way to play tit-for-tat under the title of counseling. It's not fair to the folks. And it's not fair to those of us who want to keep our feelings private."

"Do you think it's okay for you to speak for what's fair to the others in your family?" Gloria asked.

Rod rolled his eyes upward. "Are you going to ask me a question after every comment I make?"

"I will if it helps you sort your way to the bottom of the pile and find the exact problems you have to recognize in order to solve them."

"Okay, then it's probably not right for me to say what's fair for the others. But I don't think it's fair to expose *me* to these rag sessions!"

"So you're resentful of having to sit in on the counseling sessions?" Gloria asked.

"Yeah! I didn't want to come from the beginning!" Rod snapped back.

"Then why do you come to them?"

"Because the judge said we were supposed to and it might help Dad get sober!"

"You do admit then that your father's drinking does cause problems in the family's life?"

"I'd be a fool not to admit it," came Rod's reply.

"But you don't think that the judge's sending you to counseling and the possibility of helping your dad are good enough reasons to attend counseling?"

"Yes, I do." Rod's voice had an edge of exasperation in it.

"Then what's the problem?" Gloria surprised Rod with her bluntness.

He sputtered, "Me having to sit in the middle of it all, that's the problem!"

"What would you do about your problems if you hadn't been in counseling with your whole family?"

"Nothing."

"Do you think that's wise?"

"What's the difference? I don't want to be here, but I'm

forced to. There's nothing I can do about it."

"Do you suppose that the real problem underneath all this is that you feel out of control and forced to face what you don't want to?"

"Could be."

"Rod, tell me, at this minute—what are you feeling?"

Rod slapped his hands down on the arms of the chair in which he was sitting. "I'm feeling bitter, put upon and mad! Why?"

"Because you have a right to feel *whatever* you are feeling. And I've gotten the impression over these last weeks that you've taken on a role in your family that may be burdensome and unrealistic for you. I observe you trying to stop the flow of emotions when they start. I see you trying to stuff some of the things that have come out back into an invisible sack of some sort. Rod, I'd like to see you let go of some of the pressure you feel because you hold back your true feelings. Do you think that's reasonable?"

"I think that you should mind your own business!"

"Your feelings are my business—I'm your counselor."

"No! You're the family's counselor! Maybe I get my feelings out elsewhere—like with friends or in my writing for the paper! Have you ever considered that?!"

"Rod, if you express your feelings to others or through your writing, that's wonderful. And if you choose not to open up in counseling, that is certainly your right. I am trying to ask questions to help you recognize that you may have trouble expressing your true feelings to these immediate family members, and that there might be a healthier way for you to relate to them."

"I feel like I relate just fine and I don't need you to stick your nose into my life! I don't need you to tell me what I should say or not say to my parents! I don't need you to tell me about God or anyone else! I don't need you to tell

me what an alcoholic is or how I should define my problems! I just want to float these gripe meetings out and get
on with my life!"

Gloria looked at Rod closely. He was red in the face
and sweating. He was withdrawing. She nodded at him.
"All right, Rod. We'll move on to Melanie. But I would like
to give you a possible reason for why it seems easier to
just let things remain the same in your family network.

"Often, when there are problems that have gone on for
years in a family's dynamics, a point is reached in which
each member of the family assumes a defined role and
there is an uneasy truce. The role each takes may be different at different times in everyone's life. For instance, as
the youngest child, you may, at one time or another, have
taken on the personality that has traditionally entertained
the others in your family. Or, you may have run interference and seemingly kept the peace by being the one to say
there's not really a problem with your family. Or, you may
believe that since your dad didn't mean to hurt you, his
drinking and abuse is okay. If you say things like this, you
can often quiet the others down, avoid confrontations, and
therefore bypass getting in the middle of any emotional
interactions that may feel risky or messy to you. Emotions
can be messy—it's not necessarily pleasant to cry, get
angry or be resentful. But these things are reality. You
wouldn't know what it's like to laugh and be happy or joyful
if the down side didn't exist.

"It often appears easier to just let the status quo stand
for three reasons:

"One, it may appear that if you let the cap off your
emotions they'll never stop coming out, and people usually
find that very frightening.

"Two, it's all you know. It feels easier to stay with the
familiar than to risk a change, but often this just isn't true.

Change keeps us going and growing!

"Three, you may have a deep-seated fear that if your family members knew what you really thought or felt about them they'd reject you—they'd possibly not love you anymore.

"I'll leave you, Rod, with those thoughts and get on to you, Melanie." Melanie straightened in her chair. Rod looked relieved to have Gloria's attention directed elsewhere.

"You wondered why you don't get promotions at work, seem to end up dating men that are bad for you, feel the need to shock others, and why you are defensive a lot of the time. Has this week turned up any new reasons why these things are problems in your life?"

Melanie seemed to pull herself away from some far-off place. "Well, yeah, actually I have thought of a couple things. It's like I sabotage myself subconsciously. If I end up on the short end of the stick at work, with men, or in others' opinions of me, then I don't have to risk success. And I think I get so defensive because deep inside I know I'm capable of doing more with my life than I'm doing. So when anyone criticizes me, it's as if my insides screech out that they're wrong about the way they see me."

Gloria smiled widely. "What a *delightful* breakthrough! I think that you've really had some important discoveries about yourself this week! What you say—"

Gloria was interrupted by Jill muttering something. "Jill, did you have something to say that can't wait until your turn?"

"You bet I do! Little Miss Perfect Soul-Searcher of the Year leaves out one thing—she's an *alcoholic!*"

"Like h——— I am!" Melanie raged back. "What gives you a license to decide who's an alcoholic anyway? Just because I go out a lot doesn't mean I drink too much!"

"Melanie, don't be a fool!" Cole added his two cents. "You drink all the time. You can't even get through a couple hours of visiting at Mom and Dad's without hitting the bottle!"

"Oh, really, Cole? And when have you had the occasion to notice that? You're never at the family visits any more!"

Cole's voice was patronizing. "Melanie, Shel's told me how you two sneak off by yourselves for drinks when you're there together!"

"Yeah!" Jill chimed in again. "And Shel told me how you take liquor from Dad's cabinet and replace what you poured out with water. And how you have that little flask you carry in your purse for work. You even forgot one at my house—it's right in my kitchen drawer. You probably didn't even miss it!"

Melanie looked stricken and pained. Her bottom lip quivered. She appeared to be considering how to react and trying to control her emotions at the same time.

Gloria asked her calmly, "Melanie, would you care to comment on what your brother and sister just said?"

"Oh! Would I!" Melanie made a decision quickly. "Has it ever occurred to either one of you that the stories you're quoting and the things that you've heard have one thing in common? Just figure it out! I think there's a couple of much bigger fools than me in this room! I think I'm the *only* person in this family who's being honest with the rest of you and myself!"

"What are you saying, Melanie?" Gloria could feel a time bomb ticking.

"I'm saying—" Melanie looked hard at Cole, "that *Shel* is the common source! She's the one who sneaks off for drinks, refills liquor bottles and leaves flasks at Jill's house—not me. Cole, you said that Shel has been sober for a month. Well, I'm not trying to hurt you, but you need

Often the one or few who dare to speak the truth of the family's problem are at least temporarily alienated from some part of the family. They're commonly seen as the ones who "break up the family unit."

to know that I saw her at a bar last weekend, and believe me, she was anything but sober! You've got some real problems on your hands, Cole, and my being an alcoholic is not one of them!"

Cole looked as though he would be physically ill. He stared at Melanie. Then he looked at Gloria. He jumped out of his seat and burst out of the office.

"You witch, Melanie!" Jill screamed at her sister. "You selfish little witch!"

Jill got up to follow Cole, but Rod held an arm out like a parent braking a car. "Wait. I'll go," he said.

"No!" Nora stood up. "I'm his mother. I'll go."

"Please," Gloria said firmly, "all of you stay right here. When and if Cole is ready to come back here, he will. Let him have a few moments to think things through. You can all take some time to think. Then we'll move on."

Mike was leaning back against the sofa with his chin in one hand. He looked very helpless and vulnerable. Nora patted his leg. He attempted a half-smile in her direction. Nora looked at Melanie with an emotion Gloria had seen many times before on the faces of members of alcoholic family networks. The look said, "I'm so ashamed of you. How could you reveal such secrets and weaknesses in our family?"

Gloria had seen this attitude displayed hundreds of times when one or more members of the alcoholic family network began to get healthier. Often the one or few who dare to speak the truth of the family's problems are at least temporarily alienated from some part of the family. They're commonly seen as the ones who "break up the family unit." In reality, they're like lights that shine into a very dark place—rather than breaking up the family, they help the healing process to begin. There can't be total darkness and light at the same place at the same time.

As the Martin family considered the exchanges that had just taken place, Gloria got out some notes she'd taken at a recent conference on the alcoholic family network. She read them to herself.

Some Things Must Be Faced!

Even the healthier members of the alcoholic family don't *want* to bring on the traumatic pains of going through the identification, examination, recognition and reconciliation periods of recovery. But often, they are backed into a corner and forced to bring things into the open that the others wish to keep hidden. Like the others in the family, they would prefer jumping ahead to restoration and avoiding the heart-wrenching emotions that can surface during the other stages. But because they are healthier than the rest of the family, they tend to know that certain things must come out and be faced.

Doing What Must Be Done

Recovering members of the alcoholic network can feel very much alone and isolated. They may begin to want to just stay away from family gatherings and any association with the old way of acting and reacting with their families. They may move away if they live in the same town as the rest of the family; they may stop visiting or calling as often if they live out of town; their conversations with siblings and parents may take on a hollow sound—as if to say, "I've got better things to do with my life." And they do!

Getting On with Life

One thing that is vital for recovering members to realize is that they *must* get on with their own lives regardless of what other family members choose to do with theirs. If one recovering member changes his/her behavior, then the others in the network are forced to change at least how they interact with that person. *It's inevitable: if one person in an intimate relationship changes his/her attitude and behavior, those close to him/her must adapt by changing also.* This change doesn't guarantee complete recovery for any family with alcoholism because the sad truth is, many alcoholics, spouses and adult children never make a stand for their health.

It's Worth It!

Recovering family members may have to stand against anger, disapproval, bitterness, isolation and unsettling change. But through it all the Lord will guide, strengthen and support those who call on Him. Full recovery is worth the price. And if only one member of an alcoholic family network recovers, it's still one more opportunity to break the generational cycle of a terrible disease!

Misery Does Love Company!

As recovering family members gain momentum and band together, the ones who are left are the ones needing the most help; but often they are also the ones who still deny the problems. The healthier members may be brow-beaten by those still on the vicious

merry-go-round of alcoholism. The recovering ones
may be treated as traitors—as though they are selfish
for wanting to be well. The recovering members of the
network usually don't love their family any less—in
fact, as they gain wisdom and understanding, their
love and compassion quite often deepens. Yet they
may still be treated as outcasts, and this hurts to the
quick!

Stand Your Ground!

Family members trying their hardest to keep the
recovering one down—to maintain the status quo—
can be so influential that the healthier member of the
network begins to wonder if the problem is really with
the others or with him/herself. Are the rest unstable,
or is it him/her? Recovering members may drop back
into their old ways of interacting out of a real fear of
losing their family's love and support—even if these
are compromised by the illness of alcoholism. It is
very common for those getting healthier to feel lonely,
anxious, guilty, and relieved all at the same time.

Sincere Questions

One question that's never far from the minds of members of an unrecovered or partially recovered alcoholic
family network asks, "How much do we owe each
other—particularly our parents or spouses?" Other
questions include: How much pain do we have to suffer before we have the "right" to bring all this out in
the open? Has the alcoholic suffered inside enough
already—with guilt, sorrow and self-inflicted misery?
When does our speaking out cross the line from being

helpful and compassionate in motive to selfish and revengeful?

Everyone's Responsible for Him/Herself

There are questions recovering members of the alcoholic family have to answer for themselves. It may be the first time they've taken full responsibility and control of their own lives. One thing to remember: No one is responsible or at fault for the actions, words and behaviors of anyone but him/herself. Children of alcoholics cannot cause a parent to become an alcoholic. A spouse of an alcoholic cannot make his wife drink or stop drinking. The best that a person can do is to love him/herself enough to break out of the destructive patterns.

Adult children of alcoholics needn't burn with the memories of vulgarities, adulteries, temper tantrums, abuses, ridicule or abandonment. Non-alcoholic spouses have the right to not be put through the wringer again by their adult children wanting to know why they stayed with an alcoholic spouse, why they didn't have the self-esteem to get out of a horrible situation, or why they didn't get help. And alcoholics shouldn't be made to "pay" for the hurt and strife alcoholism caused their families. But how do recovering family members work through their awful memories of incidents that brought shame and humiliation upon the family? That's a hard question with answers that don't usually come easily.

The Quest Is Different for Everyone

One member of an alcoholic family network may find

that she can work things through on her own without ever having to confront another family member. But another member may find that he just can't work things out in his own life without facing each member of his family with his thoughts and feelings. Neither is right or wrong for everyone. All of us see our lives in different shades of color. No one sees the same issue in the exact same way at the same time.

But every individual's path to health and wholeness must include the common elements of bringing the disease out into the open, recognizing individual problems and why they occur, and changing a destructive course into a constructive one!

As Gloria finished reading her notes, the office door opened and Cole stepped inside. He looked around the room at his family and said, "I'm sorry. I had to take some time to think things through."

"That's fine, Cole. It's important for you to vent your feelings. Do you feel ready to continue?"

"Yeah." Cole looked at Melanie, "I'm sorry I interrupted your part of the session."

Melanie burst into tears. She bounced up from her chair and threw her arms around Cole. "I'm sorry I said those rotten things to you, Cole, but I feel like the truth has to come out somewhere, sometime. All these months you guys have carried on about my drinking. Really, I just think we need to lay our cards out on the table and get through this junk!"

"I know," Cole said stoically. "Let's just get on with it."

"Okay, then," Gloria began carefully. "Melanie, we were talking about your self-discoveries. I was remarking on what wonderful inroads you've made. Let's go on from there. Can you think of one or two words that describe why you might be sabotaging your success at work and in relationships?"

"Sure," Melanie answered quickly. "Insecurity and fear!"

"Very likely," Gloria agreed. "Now can you think why you might have these insecurities and fears?"

"Well—" Melanie answered more slowly this time. "I've been doing a lot of thinking about this. I feel like maybe I was taught somehow that to succeed beyond the level of success of others in the family isn't acceptable. Do you know what I mean?"

"I think I might," Gloria said. "It's quite common for adult children in the alcoholic family network to sort of 'tread water' when it comes to their own lives. Often they either marry alcoholics or become alcoholics, fumble through their careers and relationships and generally accept second best in their lives. What I hear you saying, Melanie is that you've held yourself back subconsciously, until now, so that you wouldn't rise above anyone else in the family and risk jealousy or resentment. In this way you could contribute to keeping the peace. Is that right?"

"Yes!" Melanie said excitedly. "And it's such a relief to find words for it! You know, here I am dressing in all these outrageous clothes—look at this orange and royal blue paisley. Come on! I mean, it's not exactly hollering out a dress-for-success look! And I know it. But, somehow, I've never been quite able to change my own image. Now I can see a pattern—if I act or dress weird at the office, on dates and around the family then I don't have to bother. Plus, I can blame my no-progress status on the people around me. But if someone gets close enough to see that there's more underneath, I get defensive and chase them away. On the other hand, if someone puts me down because they can't see beneath the bravado, then I resent that too! Oooh! This is so exciting to realize these things!"

Melanie's thrill at being able to track her own problems was not met with any great outburst of support by her other family members. Rod looked surly. Cole looked doubtful. Jill nearly glowered at her sister. Nora seemed puzzled and Mike wondered aloud, "I'd like to know what all this has to do with my drinking!"

"What do you think, Melanie?" Gloria bounced the ball back to the young woman.

"Um—at the risk of sounding like I'm blaming you, Daddy, you haven't ever been exactly overflowing with confidence in my ability to make it on my own! I mean, you basically taught me that girls should grow up, get married and have babies. You never did like it that I got an apartment of my own after high school and worked. And you do have a tendency to make fun of me. Remember when I wanted to go to college to become a biologist? You laughed your head off and asked me whatever made me think I could be a biologist! I was so hurt! I really wanted you to tell me to go for it! There's been lots of stuff like that in my life. And men? Forget it! Nobody I ever dated was good enough in your eyes! I think I'm scared to get too close to any man—I think I'm just plain scared to get too close to anyone. I'm not real big on trust. I'm always so afraid I'll end up—" Melanie blushed bright red. Her exuberance had carried her onto dangerous ground.

"End up what?" Mike challenged.

Melanie thought for a few seconds. She rushed on, "—end up marrying someone like you!" Melanie turned to Nora quickly. "No offense, Mom! I just don't want to end up taking care of a husband that—"

Melanie looked at Jill. "Ooh!" she groaned, "I can't win for losing. See, Gloria? I have to watch every single word I say or I'm walking over somebody! It's not fair that I live in this narrow world where every issue is so sensitive!"

"What do you mean?" Gloria asked.

"She means—" Jill said sarcastically, "that she didn't want to finish saying that she wasn't going to end up with a husband like Daddy—like I did!"

"Melanie?" Gloria prodded. "Is that what you meant?"

"Yes!" Melanie almost shouted. "Yes! Yes! Yes! I'm sick to death of all this tiptoeing around! I'm tired of having to be careful not to hurt poor Jill's feelings—or Cole's or Rod's or Mom's or Daddy's. Nobody's careful about hurting mine, and I think we need to be honest anyway!"

"Why do you feel that nobody's careful about hurting your feelings, Melanie?"

"Because they can see that I'm a threat to their cozy little nest of 'everybody stay put and keep each other in line.' Don't say that Jill's husband was a jerk and put her and the kids through hell! Don't talk about Cole and Shel's problems. Heaven forbid I should say Rod has any hangups, or that Mom has buried her head in the sand. And before counseling, the word 'alcoholic' wasn't even allowed to be said at the folks' house! I mean, what's the big deal? So, we've got problems. Doesn't every family?"

"Actually, yes," Gloria acknowledged. "Part of your family's problems may have their roots in the fact that things are *not* brought out into the open. But, you must remember that that doesn't mean you're completely right, Melanie, and that the feelings of your family members aren't valid as well. Your opinion of anyone else is just that—an opinion. Each of you has your own opinions and they can be very different from one another's."

"What's the difference, then, between me saying what's only my opinion and what is the truth?" Melanie demanded to know.

"Truth must be based in fact. What you think about Jill's ex-husband—even what Jill thinks of her ex-husband—is opinion. It's a fact that he's done some things that give you cause for your opinion, but he's still a person with at least a few redeeming qualities.

"You know, Melanie," Gloria continued, "I'm so excited for you and I don't want to bring you down with too much fuss over what's right or wrong. You've discovered some things that are very right for you and at this point that's what's important! You've come a long way since that first night you were here! Through this next week, be thinking of ways you can reconcile what you know to be truth for yourself and what you can change in your behavior and attitude to make your life-style more constructive. Now, I'd like to talk with Cole about his concerns of last week."

Cole looked at Gloria with sad eyes. He spoke in a husky voice. "I don't think my concerns from our last session are very relevant now."

"Oh, but they are," Gloria insisted. "In fact, they're even more so. Let's look at the bigger picture here—you felt that your family doesn't accept Shel and puts her down all the time. You noted that you feel you have to love Shel for the rest of your life. You said you live with much guilt and an attitude that nothing good or happy lasts. I think there's a pattern. Can you see one too, Cole?"

"Yeah, I can see a pattern all right—misery and hopelessness!"

"Exactly! Cole, things aren't always as bleak as they seem. Remember that when you were young you felt as if it was your responsibility to help your mother. I want to emphasize now that there isn't a child alive who can take that kind of burden. There's absolutely nothing you could have done to stop any abuse that may have been going on in your family! Do you think you deserve your present misery?"

"Maybe."

"Why?"

"I don't know. Maybe it's a punishment for something I did or didn't do. *I don't know!*" Cole was totally frustrated.

"Let's say for a minute that you do deserve your misery. What do you think your punishment is?"

"Being stuck with Shel around my neck!"

"And where did you pick up the belief that because you were married to Shel you were stuck with her behavior?" Gloria nudged.

"At home, of course," Cole stated as if it were the most obvious thing in the world.

"Please tell me how you learned this," Gloria pressed.

Cole's emotions began overflowing. "I learned it from my mother! She taught us kids that we should love Dad no matter how rotten and mean he treated us! We had to treat Grandma, *his* alcoholic mother, with respect—even with all the garbage she handed out to us! You know—I came home with a couple of buddies after a football game once and my grandmother was passed out in the middle of our living room floor—half-dressed! If you've never been embarrassed before that'll do the trick! Then there's the time she got plastered on Christmas morning and ruined everything when us kids were little! Jeez, the old biddy— I'm glad she's dead!"

Mike was across the coffee table before Gloria could do anything. He swung a punch and blood spurted from Cole's nose. "Don't you ever, *ever* speak of your grandmother like that again as long as you live! You brat! Look at you—I kept a roof over your head, clothes on your back and food in your belly for thirty years and this is the thanks I get!"

As Mike yelled, Nora, Jill, Rod and Melanie cowered deep in their seats. Their faces drained of color and no one said a word. Gloria cut in firmly. "Mike! Please sit down! I will not tolerate such abuse in my office!"

Mike spun around and glared at Gloria. "*You*, Missy, will not tell me how to treat my family! I've had all I'm gonna take out of you! Come on, Nora, we're leaving!"

"Do you think that's wise?" Gloria asked levelly.

"You bet it's wise! I'm sorry I ever fell into any of this! I sit here all these weeks, spill my guts out and then listen to my children bad-mouth me! No more! And for your information, if I want to drink, I will. No judge, no shrink, no wife and no kid will stop me! Nora! I said come on!"

Nora looked at Gloria. Her eyes were full of pleading and terror. Gloria couldn't tell if Nora was hoping Gloria would keep still or intervene. Gloria chose a middle ground. "Mike, I'd be very grateful if you'd take a few moments to go out in the hall and cool off before you leave. I'd hate for your temper to get out of hand again and cause an accident."

Mike's face turned deep, angry red. He was livid. "Oh, you'd like me to go to the hall like a kid sent out for detention? No such luck, sweetie! I said come *on*, Nora!"

Nora looked around at her children. Melanie was clasping her hands in her lap so hard her knuckles were white. Jill was chewing on her fingernails. Rod was staring at the floor. Cole held his shirt sleeve to his bleeding nose and looked challengingly at his father. Nora knew the signs. She was not about to challenge Mike in front of an outsider and risk breaking up the family completely over this. She reacted as she always had before. "Okay, Mike, let's go."

The couple left the room. Gloria's heart was heavy over what had just transpired. She hoped she could keep the four adult children there together to try to talk things out—even if it took all night. She went to her desk, pulled tissues from a box and handed them to Cole. He pushed part of one up a nostril and wiped at his shirt with the others.

"I'm sorry," Cole started, "I shouldn't have said what I did. I should've known he'd get like that."

"Should've! Should've! Should've!" Melanie piped up. "Who makes the rules anyway? We let this one man dictate what we should and shouldn't do in our lives! What's the deal? He can't cope with his own problems—why would we trust him to help us with ours?"

"Because he's our father," Rod said simply.

"Whoopee!" Jill sniped. "Our father—what kind of father has he been, Rod? Like he was really there to help us grow up! It's about time we faced some facts for our own lives! Look at me! Here I am—35 years old and I act like a scared dog when Daddy just raises his voice—like I was 10 again! This isn't right!"

"Knock it off, Jill," Rod said. "You're getting crazy as a loon over all this."

"Oh? And you're not? Maybe you were too young to remember the worst of it. How many times did you have to help Daddy to bed when he was too drunk to walk? How many times did Mom send you into the bathroom to clean up his puke because she had to baby him to sleep so he wouldn't get in a rage and hurt somebody? How many times did you bring home four *A*'s and a *B* on your report card and have Daddy holler at you for getting the *B* without ever saying a word about the *A*'s? Crazy as a loon? I probably am! I've spent my whole life trying to be good enough at something just to get his approval—or *somebody's* approval! I made sure I was the best wife, the best mother, the best neighbor, the best church worker, the best everything. And what has it gotten me? A whole lot of misery—that's what! I've got two half-grown kids who think it's normal to be party animals because their grandpa and dad are such fine examples! I'll pay for this booze thing the rest of my life! When will it ever end?" Jill looked pleadingly into Gloria's eyes.

"When you stop letting it *control* your life," Gloria said softly.

"Stop letting it control my life!" Jill shrieked. "How can I do that? I have anxiety attacks so bad that before I leave the house to come here I'm in the bathroom throwing up and having the runs. How do I stop that, Gloria? I have to take tranquilizers just to get through a holiday with my family. I can't sleep at night. I've taken all the responsibility for my own family—husband, kids and me—for 15 years and what's it gotten me? It's gotten me sick, lonely, depressed, angry and phobic! How far do I have to go before *someone* will love me just for being me?"

Gloria winced at the desolation in Jill's voice. She tried to get through to the panic-stricken woman. "Jill, please listen carefully—I know you're upset right now, but try— others *do* love you for who you are, or at least they will, after *you* begin to really love yourself. I promise you that you can get better. You *can* be a whole person!"

Tears ran down Jill's face. She was gulping for air and visibly shaking. "A whole person?" she hiccupped. "A whole person? Right now I'd settle for being half a person!"

Cole and Melanie went to Jill and put their arms around her. "It's okay, Jillie," Melanie crooned. "It's okay. You're gonna be fine."

Rod remained where he was, sullen and unyielding. Gloria looked at him. "Rod, can you tell me what you're feeling right now?"

"Nothing," he said. "Absolutely nothing. There's been

so much emotion the last few weeks, I'm just plain numb."

Gloria nodded. "Cole and Melanie, please sit back down now. Let's try to sort some things through before we end our session. What do you guys think about your parents leaving like they did? Cole?"

"It's a usual reaction for them. Dad acts like an animal and Mom tries to do what she thinks he wants her to do so he'll settle down."

"What do you think happened after they left here?"

"That's easy! They're driving home. He's yelling at Mom about what rotten little brats we all grew up to be and how he can't understand it 'cause he's given his whole life to keeping his family together. Mom's just staring into the dark—hopefully at an angle that won't make him think she's trying to ignore or challenge him. When they get home he'll go to the liquor cabinet and grab out his scotch. She'll try to sneak off to do something else. He'll holler at her to stay with him. If she's lucky he'll have a couple of drinks and say, 'Oh, the h—- with it! I don't know what's wrong with you people!' and go to bed. If she's not lucky, he'll keep her up all night—drinking and yakking about how awful the rest of the world is. Once in awhile he'll slobber out that he's not perfect, but at least he tries. That's what's going on with them."

"And is that how it goes with you and Shel?" Gloria surprised Cole by switching directions.

He looked at her with sorrow in his eyes. "Naw—Shel spends too much time trying to hide her drinking. When she's plastered she just cries about how horrible she is and how she doesn't know how I can love her and a whole bunch of junk like that."

"How do you react to that?" Gloria asked.

"I usually just tell her she's wrong and that she's a good wife and I do love her."

"Is she a good wife—and do you love her?"

"Ha! No, she's not a good wife and I don't know if I love her!"

"But you feel stuck with her because you were taught how a marriage 'should be' by watching your own parents live in a less-than-fulfilling relationship?"

"I guess," Cole shrugged.

"What do you mean, you guess?" Gloria inquired.

"Well, technically I know that my parents' marriage isn't necessarily an example for me to follow, but what my head says is right and what my growing up taught me are two different things. It's pretty hard to just wipe out the old habits."

"What old habits are you referring to?" Gloria asked.

"Like putting up with Shel's behavior. Remember, I've been to counseling on my own. I know I shouldn't tolerate the way she acts with her drinking, but it's hard to do anything about it—I mean she *is* my wife!"

"Does that make you responsible for her well-being?"

"No—" Cole hesitated, "but it makes me obligated to her."

"In what way?"

"To stay married!" Cole acted shocked that Gloria would even ask.

"And if you don't like your job, if your boss punches you in the nose and verbally attacks you, will you stick with it anyway?"

"No."

"Then tell me the difference with Shel—if she won't help herself, if she abuses you and your relationship—why do you stay with her?"

"*Because,*" Cole was exasperated. "I married her for better or for worse! If I leave her, I'd be walking out on something just because the going got tough! That's not right! My other counselor told me about this mother of an alcoholic daughter. The mother tried hard not to bail her daughter out of the messes she got herself into. The mother tried to block out the daughter and not worry about her—just leave it up to God. But the mother said it was like being a mother bird and trying to push the last baby out of the nest but the baby just wouldn't go. Or if the mother did get it out, the baby bird just fell to the ground. The mother couldn't let the neighborhood cat eat her young, so she'd swoop down and save it—the mother bird just couldn't finish her mothering job because her baby was weak and helpless. That's how I feel about Shel."

"But Shel isn't a baby," Gloria said. "I am not suggesting you leave her. I just don't want you to 'baby' Shel or rescue her or feel trapped. If you can recognize that you *choose* to be there, it may give you feelings of freedom and security that can help you to make your marriage to Shel better!

"You'll have to remember that God gave both of you free will. Just as you are free to affirm your choice to stay married, give Shel the freedom to take responsibility for her own behavior. God loves her enough to let her learn her own lessons. And He loves you enough to help you implement the changes that are necessary to keep your marriage intact if that's His will!

"Now, Cole, let me ask you *why* you resent your family for seemingly not accepting Shel."

"Because I want them to understand and love her!"

"And why do you feel guilty over how *you* feel about Shel?" Gloria continued.

"I shouldn't have these rotten feelings toward her! Not if I'm a good husband!"

"So, you not only choose to stay in a miserable situation and put up with unacceptable behavior, but you also expect the others in your family to tolerate it. *And* you expect yourself to like it?"

"Well, no," Cole looked confused. "Huh! I get it—I can't have everything?"

"I asked you," Gloria responded. "What do you think?"

"I think I've gotten myself into a real jam!" Cole said with a sigh.

"And how do you think you might get out of it?" Gloria would not let go.

"I guess I either leave Shel or change my attitude toward my situation."

"What else? What can you do if you stay with Shel to make your life easier?"

"Get on with my own stuff, I guess. Ignore her?" Cole asked sincerely.

"Well, you're getting on the right track. You think that through this next week. I want you all to think about the things that went on tonight. You've made some excellent headway into recognizing the sources of your various problems. You've recognized many different reasons for why you act and react to your lives the way you do. I'm proud of you!

"Melanie, I want you to think about developing the courage to strive to reach your potential. You know, your success may affect your family in a way that is opposite of how you think it will—your success may free other members of your family to get healthier and stronger. Seeing you change your own image may be just what they need to give them hope.

"Cole, I want you to carefully think through your relationship with Shel. Don't be afraid to let her know that *you* have needs. Talk about what you want your future to be, and how she can fit into that future. It won't hurt you to be self-caring. Sometimes there's a fine line between selfishness and love of self. Search for your line and check out how you might feel on either side!"

Gloria turned to Jill. "I want you to do a similar thing this week. Attempt to recognize the disadvantages in trying to be the very best at everything all the time. Look at where it's gotten you and imagine the worst that could happen if you were lousy at some things sometimes. Jill, you be self-focused this week, too. Daydream about where you'd like your life to take you and how you honestly feel about your family.

"Rod, please consider the benefits of allowing the lid to come off your emotions for a little while. Imagine the harm that may come from keeping your feelings inside and tolerating this numbness you're experiencing versus the long-range good that could come from opening up.

"Next week we'll look at ways everyone can begin to change from destructive to constructive behavior patterns. We'll see how acceptance, understanding, knowledge and wisdom can be anchors to keep you healthy and full of inner joy and peace. You *can* all experience a full recovery from your alcoholic family network background!

"God has placed inside each of us the ingredients for a sound mind. Second Timothy 1:7 says, 'For God did not give us a spirit of timidity, but a spirit of power, of love and of self-discipline.' You can overcome your problems and struggles—you can use them to enrich your lives with wisdom and understanding. You can allow them to give you depth of character and gentleness of spirit!

Exercise Five

Mapping Your Reaction Patterns: Circumstances

On paper, map the cycles of your negative reactions to common circumstances, events, and relationships. See the following maps for examples.

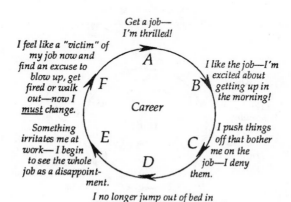

Get a job—I'm thrilled!

I feel like a "victim" of my job now and find an excuse to blow up, get fired or walk out—now I __must__ change.

I like the job—I'm excited about getting up in the morning!

A

F

B

Career

Something irritates me at work—I begin to see the whole job as a disappointment.

E

C

I push things off that bother me on the job—I deny them.

D

I no longer jump out of bed in the morning—I drag in to work.

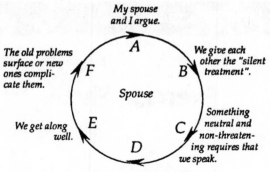

My spouse
and I argue.

A

The old problems
surface or new
ones compli-
cate them.

F

We give each
other the "silent
treatment".

B

Spouse

We get along
well.

E

Something
neutral and
non-threaten-
ing requires that
we speak.

C

D

We give in to our need for
contact and peace, and we
call a truce.

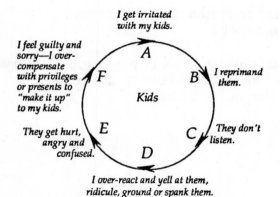

I get irritated
with my kids.

A

I feel guilty and
sorry—I over-
compensate
with privileges
or presents to
"make it up"
to my kids.

F

I reprimand
them.

B

Kids

They get hurt,
angry and
confused.

E

They don't
listen.

C

D

I over-react and yell at them,
ridicule, ground or spank them.

I drink.

A

Something irri-
tating, unpleas-
ant or "worth
celebrating"
happens.

F

I feel sick and
guilty later.

B

Alcohol

I begin to feel
edgy— I want to
drink.

E

I try to "make
up" to my family
or friends by
being extra nice and
considerate.

C

D

The pressure of being so
"nice" wears on me.

Look over your own maps. Do you see repeated in each diagram a point at which your ability to follow through with healthy reactions breaks down? Do you cause an argument, quit a job, take a drink, ridicule your children or get depressed at the same stage on each map?

Do these incidents happen at similar times, such as when you feel threatened, insecure, angry, jealous, irritated, frustrated or helpless? If so, think of parallel situations from your childhood. When an alcoholic parent got thoroughly frustrated or threatened, did he/she resort to ridicule, stony silence or physical power plays? Did your parents argue at about the same stage of interaction as you do with your spouse now? Do you believe it is "normal" for couples to be extremely jealous about one another and to find yourself unable to get past jealousy in some areas of your relationship?

What to Do

Here's how you can begin to break the cycle of your negative reactions and make some new maps for yourself:

1. *Be aware!* Just before you reach a point where you see that your reactions usually break down in an argument, a name-calling session, walking out on a job or a fist fight—stop yourself cold. Take ten deep breaths, silently telling yourself to inhale and exhale as you do each.

2. *Be committed!* If you are still emotionally distraught after you've taken ten deep breaths, excuse yourself from the room and go to the bathroom or break room at work, your bedroom at home, or outdoors. Learn to control your emotions so that they will not control you. After a few minutes of thought and prayer for strength, go back to the situation. Start a conversation all over again if you have to in order to remap your reaction cycle.

3. *Be persistent!* Don't allow setbacks to stop you from trying again and again. If you lose your temper during an exchange, stop. Tell the person(s) you're interacting with that you're sorry and would like to begin the communication again. If you've gotten drunk after a few days, weeks or months of sobriety, remind yourself that you're human and you make mistakes. Then set an immediate goal to start your sobriety again. Begin again as many times as it takes to break the cycle of your negative reactions and responses to events, relationships, and circumstances.

4. *Be excited!* You can do it! You can change your maps of negative reactions, and relate in a healthy way to yourself, others and life! Change may come slowly and with great effort, but it *will* come. When it does, your self-esteem, joy and inner peace will be multiplied many, many times over. Don't underestimate yourself. Pray that God will help you and lead you. You have every reason in the world to be excited about your future!

Stage 4

RECONCILIATION

Changing destructive behavior into constructive living
by gaining knowledge, understanding, acceptance
and wisdom.

Beginning to Set Things Right

When the Martin family arrived for their sixth counseling session, Gloria was sorry to see that Nora and Mike were not with their children. After last week's outburst, Gloria wasn't surprised. However, she had hoped that Mike would push beyond the problem and move forward on his own to begin the reconciliation stage with the rest of the family. Now Gloria would have to use the authority of the judge's court order to try and get Mike and Nora back on track with their counseling. She didn't like to do that, but Mike did not leave her a choice.

Jill, Cole, Melanie and Rod seemed more relaxed without their parents present—this didn't surprise Gloria either. It is common for the adult children of alcoholics to be very nervous around their drinking—or newly sober—parent(s). This stems from being subjected to years of unpredictable and inconsistent behavior in their lives. When the parents aren't around, adult children can act like themselves without the threat of being yelled at, ridiculed or physically abused.

Gloria glanced at Rod. He looked sullen, as he had the last two or three sessions. This worried Gloria because at the start of counseling Rod had exhibited a quick sense of humor and some desire to cooperate. Now he seemed just the opposite. As some of the emotional issues of his family's problems were revealed, he withdrew and reacted negatively. This was not a good sign. What might reach Rod? He seemed to be the kind of adult child who could not express—or maybe he didn't know—what he really felt deep inside. Gloria decided to continue watching Rod closely for places where he might be ready for help.

Gloria greeted the four Martins and started the session. "I want to tell you about a former client of mine. I'll call her Jeanne. Jeanne's mother was severely alcoholic. Her parents divorced when she was in grade school. Jeanne had to learn how to manage an entire household when she was just a child. Sometimes she even forged her mother's signature on checks when a delivery came to the house because dear old mom was passed out on the couch.

"Jeanne became bitter and lonely over the years. When she was a teenager she began dating all the wrong kinds of boys—boys she knew her mother would hate. This 'I got you!' routine continued throughout Jeanne's high school years. But it backfired on her as a young adult.

"Her pattern of dating men that weren't good for her continued long after she should have outgrown the need to pay her mother back. Jeanne dated men who were needy in a variety of ways. But she was still needy herself. By dating men who were unable to make healthy decisions for themselves regarding careers, love or leisure, Jeanne assured herself a place in their hearts. She could be depended upon—just as she'd run her mother's household as a child, she now orchestrated the lives of the men she dated. The kinds of men that were drawn to her stuck like glue. Her relationships were a kind of sick security blanket that worked on behalf of all concerned.

"Eventually, however, Jeanne lost respect for each of her dating partners and then found herself seeing them with the same kind of disgust she had felt for her mother.

"Besides troubled relationships, Jeanne also had various compulsive behaviors and physical symptoms. She smoked heavily, she ate too many of the wrong kinds of food and got fat, she drank to get drunk when she went out, and she became sexually dysfunctional."

In a high-pitched voice, Jill interrupted Gloria's story with, "What do you mean—sexually dysfunctional?"

"I mean that she was unable to enjoy sex. In counseling we discovered that she felt tremendous guilt and shame because she had been with so many men. When she was with one man, her mind wandered to visions of others she'd been with. Negative feelings multiplied to the point at which sex became a burden rather than a pleasure. When Jeanne eventually married, she couldn't enjoy a natural sexual relationship with her husband, due to the haunting memories of her past. She pretended to be fulfilled in their encounters and happy with their sex life. Her pretense contributed more to the mushrooming of guilt, shame and frustration which controlled Jeanne's life by then.

"Jeanne acted out a pattern of what I call 'angry consumption.' Her habits, or any of yours in which you tend to be compulsive or 'over-consuming,' are clues to areas of your life where you're not taking responsibility for yourself—for your own well-being. If 'angry consumption' habits are left unchecked they can lead to depression, illness or even death.

"For example, smoking, overeating, sexual promiscuity, heavy drinking, using illegal drugs, driving recklessly, or anything you do too much of or too often, can be harmful to you. Things that make you feel guilty, upset, blameful, envious, self-pitying, helpless, disappointed or angry quite often are clues that there's something in your life that's keeping you in a destructive holding pattern.

"Jeanne was able to fully recover from growing up with alcoholism. But first she closely examined the areas in her life where she was feeling upset, guilty, helpless and ashamed.

"She realized that her behavior indicated she had hateful feelings toward herself. She began to see that the things she'd done to get back at her mother were, in truth, against herself."

Gloria looked directly into the eyes of each of the Martin adult children before she continued. "Know this—it is good and right and natural for each of you to love yourself. By loving yourself, you will automatically begin to nurture yourself! It is reasonable and healthy to expect those close to you to help love and nurture you. Sometimes it's difficult to convince people who've grown up with destructive life-styles that this is true. Sometimes they feel that to watch out for themselves is self-indulgent and wrong, but I'm here to tell you that you'd *better* begin to learn to love yourself, because your very life may depend on it!

"Continue to identify, examine and look for motives behind the feelings and behaviors that give you trouble. Then look for the 'pay-offs' of your feelings and behaviors. Jeanne realized that her overeating, smoking, sexual promiscuity and dangerous drinking habits kept her in a narrow world and allowed her to avoid taking responsibility for her own happiness. If she got fat, she could blame the fact that she wasn't attractive enough—in her own eyes—to magnetize a healthy man into her life. Building

We must love ourselves enough
to honestly examine our lives and
break through the confining barriers of
addictions and destructive behaviors.

and responding to healthy relationships is work. Jeanne had grown up in an unhealthy relationship with her mother. *That* was hard work! She subconsciously envisioned healthy ones to be even harder.

"Jeanne used her low opinion of herself as a twisted excuse to have sex as recreation. She thought she might just as well sleep around because no 'good' man would want her. She confused sex with love, and love at any price or for any reason was better than no love at all. Besides, being able to give or withhold something a man desired from her in this most intimate of circumstances was one of the few situations where Jeanne felt she had some control.

"Jeanne kept smoking because cigarettes were her 'friends'—she thought. They never let her down, they didn't criticize her, they were always there, she controlled how she used them—even if that was compulsively—and they allowed her to sit and get a handle on her emotions. The pay-off was not risking change in her life and not confronting the very difficult challenge to quit smoking.

"Her last compulsive behavior epitomized her miserable cycle. She'd drink when her life became too unhappy to bear, until she no longer cared.

"We must love ourselves enough to honestly examine our lives and break through the confining barriers of addictions and destructive behaviors. Jeanne's pay-offs all fell into one main category—they kept her from risking healthy change. In her mind she could justifiably stay unhappy, unsatisfied and helpless.

"Jeanne needed to love herself! To get her pointed in the right direction, I asked her to make a list of what she thought she wanted out of life at that time. The things she listed were to be only about herself—having nothing to do with her mother, husband, any future children or anyone else. All she could come up with, the first time we did this, was that she wanted to get a 25-cent an hour raise at work—no aspirations of changing careers, going to college, gaining freedom from her destructive behaviors, or getting control of her life.

"I hoped that, like a grain of sand that eventually turns into a pearl, this desire could begin to build up Jeanne's self-esteem.

"I had Jeanne list ways to achieve her goal. She came up with two: she could ask her boss outright for the raise or, since she was a waitress, she could ask to work a busier shift so that her tips would cover her desired increase of income.

"Once Jeanne listed her options, I told her it was very important that she act on her choice as soon as possible. Acting on a choice or decision we've made helps us to gain a foothold in controlling our lives. Jeanne asked to change shifts. She didn't have enough self-confidence to bluntly ask for a raise. She was told that it wasn't possible for her to switch to the busier shift. She tried to let it drop at that. But counseling demands accountability—Jeanne didn't want me to keep asking her about acting on her options. After her next session with me, she stammered out to her boss that she wanted a raise. He turned her down. Jeanne didn't act disappointed or surprised—she figured it was just par for the course of her life.

"It's common for members of an alcoholic family network to settle for less than they hope for and to think that they don't deserve better.

"Jill, you've had problems in feeling like you have to be the best at things in order to get approval. But in striving to be the best, you commit yourself to so many obligations that you can't possibly meet them all well. This way you have a built-in excuse to do your best *or* fail—whichever suits the occasion. So you don't have to strive for real excellence at any one thing—you can just pretend you're stuck with what you get.

"Cole, you have said you feel 'stuck' with Shel and even with being miserable. Has it ever occurred to you that the pay-off for maintaining the status quo is that you don't have to be responsible for your own happiness? Have you considered how handy it is to always have someone available to take the blame for your unhappiness? Shel is apparently enmeshed in her alcoholism, so it's fairly easy to blame things on her. Could this be a possible pay-off pattern for your personal problems?"

Cole looked shocked at the thought. He grunted something that sounded like, "Maybe." Gloria wasn't ready for any real interaction with or between the siblings yet so she quickly turned to Melanie.

"Melanie, you seem to have an 'all-or-nothing' attitude too—just like your brothers and sister. You've felt that you're always the butt of your family's jokes, that you always get passed over for promotions and always get hooked up with the wrong men. We've talked about your flamboyant style of dress as being a way for you to avoid really taking off for success. Again, the pay-off is that if you never have the opportunity to win, you don't have to face losing. Consistent failure allows you to stay in the same, defeating patterns.

"And Rod, your not facing or dealing with the issues of your alcoholic family network is also an all-or-nothing facade. In essence, you're saying, 'If I have to deal with it all I just won't deal with it!' You know, I was thinking when you first came in tonight about what a pleasant sense of humor you had the first couple of sessions and how somber you've gotten over the past weeks. Please consider that the reason may be this all-or-nothing attitude. Have you decided that if it can't be your way, it simply won't be?

"Members of alcoholic families quite often see things in this destructive black-or-white mind-set. We can rid ourselves of all-or-nothing attitudes! One of the best ways to get rid of the habits that affirm these attitudes is to channel the energy we use to stay in destructive behavior patterns into harmless avenues. I'll use Jeanne's example again. She believed that her life was one big pile of garbage, and that there just wasn't any hope for her. She thought that getting turned down for a raise was just typical of the dismal course of her life.

"I began working with Jeanne to help her channel her compulsive and rebellious tendencies without risking her health and well-being. We devised a plan in which she could do one compulsive thing and one rebellious thing each day—as long as each was healthy and constructive. She came to her weekly counseling sessions with a list of the things she'd done daily. For instance, one week she ate four carrots each day for her compulsive behavior and didn't make her bed for her rebellious behavior.

"This may sound silly. The truth is that choosing two things to do gave Jeanne a way to challenge herself, get creative and really think about her behavior. Her good compulsive behaviors, like eating carrots, gave her momentum. She soon began losing a little weight, which gave her more momentum, and she went on a healthy diet. She lost more weight.

One week she switched her compulsive behavior to physical exercise. Each time she felt a negative emotion she went to her bedroom, or the storage room at work, and did five quick calisthenics. Over a period of months, she really started looking fit!

"On the other hand, her rebellious behaviors allowed her to feel like she had a little more say in what was going on in her life. And it didn't harm anything not to make her bed.

"I had a male client who used his choice of rebellious behavior in another way—he rebelled against and let go of old hurts by doing things he'd always wanted to do or was never allowed to do as a child and young adult.

"For example, his parents had been fanatics about his not tying up the phone when he was a teenager. He allowed himself 30 minutes of leisurely phone conversation with a friend or relative every night. It didn't take him very long to feel that he had control in this area of his life and let go of the bitter memory he'd stored in his mind. This rebellious behavior dropped by the wayside naturally in a few weeks.

"With their new, constructive behavior patterns, both Jeanne and this man were making wonderful friendships— friendships with themselves. The key was spending time on themselves! Each of us needs to do this for total health! We need to care enough to think about ourselves. *Why* do we do the things we do? What can we do about the things that are destructive to our well-being? How can we channel destructive behavior into constructive, harmless activity? By spending quality time in our own company, we can begin to nurture and love ourselves fully. Nurturing activities can include things like reading good books, swimming, riding horses, learning a new hobby, gardening, playing the piano, or any number of things that we've either forgotten how to take pleasure in or want to learn to enjoy now!

"We'll talk more about this at your last counseling session. Right now, I want to list four ways to help you think about your problems and what you can do about them:

"One, be patient with yourself. It isn't realistic to think your behavior will change overnight and you'll never again do any of the old things you don't like about yourself. In Romans 7:15 Paul says, 'I do not understand what I do. For what I want to do I do not do, but what I hate I do.' Again, realize that you are a human being with weaknesses and faults. There will be times when you know very well you're doing what you shouldn't, and still go ahead with it anyway. Producing the fruit of the Spirit takes time and processing—sometimes a whole lifetime isn't enough in some areas of our lives—but you must keep trying!

"Two, accept the challenges and hardships of this lifetime with gladness, if you can. James 1:2-5 says, 'Consider it pure joy, my brothers, whenever you face trials of many kinds, because you know that the testing of your faith develops perseverance. Perseverance must finish its work so that you may be mature and complete, not lacking anything. If any of you lacks wisdom, he should ask God, who gives generously to all without finding fault, and it will be given to him.'

"Three, notice it says that God gives 'to all without finding fault.' You can't earn it, succeed at it, accomplish it, or buy it, but His love is there no matter how bad you feel or how badly you mess up! Romans 8:1, 2 say, 'Therefore, there is now no condemnation for those who are in Christ Jesus, because through Christ Jesus the law of the Spirit of life set me free from the law of sin and death.' You see, it doesn't matter what kind of background you come from. If your heart is willing, He will help you change your life. You can reconcile your problems to solutions, your past to your present and future, and your doubts to confidence!

"Four, when you get tired and afraid, remember Isaiah 41:10: 'So do not fear, for I am with you; do not be dismayed, for I am your God. I will strengthen you and help you; I will uphold you with my righteous right hand.'

***

Gloria smiled at the Martins. She said, "I'd like you each to think of constructive compulsive and rebellious behaviors that would help you with one of your own problems."

Apparently, Melanie's mind had been racing already. She squealed, "I know what I can do for my rebellion! I can wear outrageous *night* clothes!"

Everyone laughed. Gloria said, "Very good! What about a compulsive activity?"

"Hmmm," Melanie thought. "I don't know. I'll have to think some more."

Gloria turned to Jill. "How about you?"

"Well," Jill considered, "each week I could say no to one unnecessary thing that someone asks me to do."

"Good. That would be rebellion. Can you think of a compulsive activity, Jill?"

"I could replace the no to someone else with a yes for me to do something I really want to do."

"Excellent! Can you think of anything, Cole?" Gloria asked.

"Not really."

"How about being compulsive in trying to find one nice thing to say to Shel each day and rebelling by not letting Shel's behavior bother you?" Gloria suggested.

Cole contemplated this for a few seconds before answering, "Okay, I'll try that."

Gloria looked at Rod. "What might you do, Rod?"

"I don't know!" He crossed his arms on his chest.

"Maybe you could write in a journal," Gloria offered. "Each day as a compulsive activity you could write about something that's going well for you. Can you think of a rebellious one?"

"Sure," Rod grinned widely. "I can rebel by not writing in a journal at all!"

Gloria couldn't help but laugh. "Okay, you think about this on your own, Rod. The important thing is that you all realize that by participating in these activities you will begin to notice more about your behavior. Then you can begin to see what's good for you and what's bad. In order to make constructive changes in your life, you must first be aware of destructive patterns.

"This week I'd like you all to think about these two questions:

"One—who are you now?

"Two—who would you like to be, if different from who you are?

"Remember that reconciliation means to restore to harmony. As you think of the other examples I've used tonight, strive for the goal of creating or restoring harmony in your lives."

As Gloria concluded the session, she was happy to see that some of the tension usually apparent on the faces of the Martin adult children was gone. They appeared relaxed, almost relieved. Gloria went to her desk and pushed a button on her tape recorder. She turned to the Martins.

"As you all know, I tape our sessions. I'd like one of you to take tonight's cassette to your parents with a note to them. Who will do that for me?"

There were a few seconds of silence and then Melanie answered winsomely. "I will, but if Daddy belts me one, I'm sending you the doctor bill!"

Gloria smiled. "Melanie, I'll bet there's never a dull moment when you're around. Thanks for dropping this off to your parents. I really hope that they'll come next time."

Gloria slipped the cassette into an envelope with a note she'd written earlier to Mike and Nora. The note reminded them that it was important that they follow through on the judge's order for them to attend family counseling. Gloria told them she would allow this session to be made up by their listening to the tape, but that next week she genuinely hoped they would set a good example for their adult children by coming back and finishing the sessions. Gloria knew it would be hard for Mike to swallow his pride and finish counseling, but she prayed that he would.

Exercise Six

Changing Destructive Patterns into Constructive Ones
For Personal Growth

List things you really enjoy doing. Your list can include everything from watching a pretty sunset to working out at the gym. If you like to shop, play golf, decorate, design floor plans, invent things, visit with friends, swim, spend time alone, look at fine art, garden, fix up old cars, build things from wood, read, take long baths—list it! Write down *anything* that makes your heart feel good about thumping!

Next, list the things that you really dislike. If you absolutely detest doing housework, settling arguments between your children, getting stuck making coffee at work, doing fix-up chores around the house, cooking for two, folding the laundry, picking up the kids from the babysitter's, changing oil in the car, paying all the bills—that's what goes on this list. Write down anything that makes your stomach cringe when you have to do it!

What to Do

First of all, ask yourself where you may have gotten the idea that parts of life *must* be miserable or burdensome. Many people insist, "Well, life's just not a bowl of cherries!" Or, "I guess this is the way things have to be." Wait a minute! Jesus said we would have troubles on earth; He didn't say we needed to live in despair for years at a time! He said that He came so we could live abundantly—not miserably or meagerly!

There's a big difference between coping with troubles and hardship and sticking with unnecessary patterns of behavior that are destructive to your well-being! If you take care of yourself during the "easy" times of life, then you'll be better prepared for the troubles and for the mundane chores that can grind you down!

Granted, it isn't thrilling to clean the bathroom or snake out a drain, but these are mere moments in time—they aren't huge chunks out of life. At least they shouldn't be! And if they are, there's not much delegating or equal sharing of household chores going on! It is *all right* to enjoy your life to the fullest—fitting in as much constructive activity as you possibly can.

The object of this next activity is to make your list of favorite activities grow, while the list of disliked chores shrinks.

Shifting the Balance

1. Look at the list of things you *enjoy*. Do you see any patterns? For instance, swimming and yard work are physical, outdoor activities. On the other hand, reading and crocheting are sedentary activities typically done indoors. Consider whether you are mostly extroverted or introverted, spontaneous or structured.

2. You've clarified the basic outline of your personality by examining the activities you like. For example, you may see more clearly that you really enjoy demanding, physical work and hobbies. Or perhaps you've learned that you are a slower-paced individual. Whatever patterns you discover on your list can help you add to the number of activities you like and diminish the influence of the things you dislike. Brainstorm other activities available to you that are similar to or have something in common with things you like. If you like swimming and fishing, you may want to try scuba diving. If you like reading and playing Scrabble, take up crossword puzzles. There are an endless number of healthy, constructive things that you can research and sample.

Now let's look at how you can diminish the influence in your life of the things you dislike.

3. Look at the first item on the list of things you dislike. Is the item you're looking at opposite in nature to most of your likes? For instance, is the thing you dislike an indoor task, when you mostly love to be outdoors? Is the thing you dread a sedentary activity, and you long for a physical chore? Does something you hate to do require you to be socially exposed when you'd rather be alone or on a one-to-one basis with another?

4. Try to capitalize on the activities you like to do and find alternate ways to get the others done. If you hate to do housework, but love to do yard work, try to arrange the family roster of responsibilities to minimize the number of Saturdays you have to pull house duty. If you live by yourself, hire someone once a week or month to help around the house so you can spend time in the yard. If you can't afford that, trade with a neighbor who likes to putter around the house but hates to mow, pull weeds or water the flowers. The same thing goes for mechanical work on

your vehicle—if you hate to change the oil and spark plugs but don't mind painting trim or cleaning gutters, trade this type of work with a friend, neighbor or relative. If you're a gourmet cook but hate to do book work, trade around by providing casseroles, baked goods, soups, etc. in return for book work.

Try to fit some of the activities you dislike into categories that you like in general. For example, if you don't like to rake, but you do like to be outdoors, make a game of it! For every pile of leaves you rake, do something else you like to do outside. Or if you like to be sedentary, but must exercise for your health, set up a schedule of physical activities to do in conjunction with something you like. Read while you ride your stationary bike. Listen to cassette tapes as you jog. Do a few easy stretches or bends while you're in the shower.

5. Shorten your list of dislikes by asking yourself if each item is really necessary to your survival; if not, don't do it. Changing destructive behaviors to constructive behavior is often a matter of stopping a habit that isn't absolutely necessary. If it makes you nuts to turn the kids' socks right side out before they go into the washing machine, *then don't do it!* If you hate it that your spouse gets home later from work than you want to eat, then eat early. And if dinner is your family's together time, then sit at the table and visit while your spouse eats, or eat dessert together. If you can't stand the guys or girls bickering at the office or in the lunchroom, then leave the area—don't listen! It's often simply not necessary to expose ourselves to the constant irritation of things that bother us and, therefore, become destructive to our happiness.

If your alcoholic parent has ridiculed or criticized you all your life and you're half crazy from it, then tell your parent that, from now on, when he or she begins the same old ragging on you, you will leave the room or the house. *You have a choice!* You do not have to tolerate abusive, neglectful, disrespectful or destructive behavior from others! (The issue of changing destructive behavior into constructive behavior in relationships will be discussed in the next exercise.)

6. Allow yourself to change destructive behavior, which often means forcing yourself to do things you detest, into constructive and healthy behavior. Consider the points that follow:

- Believe in yourself!
- Take challenges and some common-sense risks.
- Surround yourself with a network of supportive people.
- Reach beyond your own needs and touch others.
- Accept the fact that nothing stays the same, and be willing to change for the better.
- Stay as busy as you can with things that you like.
- Be willing to laugh at the world and yourself!
- Follow your gut instincts about what's right for you.
- Try to be childlike in your attitudes and pleasures—nothing takes the place of simple wonders in nature, play and creativity!

Get Help for Big Problems

If you have destructive behaviors related to serious problems like alcohol and other drug abuse, physical abuse, sexual perversion, criminal activity or anything else that is illegal/immoral/addictive *then get professional help immediately!* There is no single book, quiz or piece of advice that can change criminal activity into honest work, or physical abuse into innocent roughhousing. If you tell whopping lies much of the time, you'd be well advised to get some counseling. If you've forced yourself sexually on your spouse, you can benefit from therapy. These are some of the things to use as a guideline to know when to get professional guidance to stop destructive behavior and learn skills for constructive living!

Finally, pray that God will help you recognize ways to get healthy and whole—to live abundantly and joyfully—and then ask for the incentive and ability to make changes! Bear in mind that your quest is not for an eternal fountain of selfish pleasure, but for one of healthy, constructive self-love. He *will* help you!

Nurturing for the Long Run

As the time drew near for the Martin family's seventh session of counseling, Gloria prayed that Mike and Nora would return and that the adult children of this alcoholic family network would report that they were making headway on some of the problems that had roots in their background.

Gloria's prayers were answered.

Melanie bounded through the door several minutes early and burst forth ecstatically, "Gloria! You won't believe what's happened! I went downtown the other day and bought a nice blue suit—you know, the kind women wear when they really want to look professional? Well! The next morning I went to my boss and told him about our counseling sessions and that I was getting a handle on some of my attitude problems. Then I asked him to consider me for the next available promotion in my department. And guess what? Oooh! I'm so excited—the lady that's been just above me is quitting in a few months because she's pregnant and the boss said that if I follow through on my new outlook, the promotion's mine! Can you believe it? I did it!"

"That's wonderful, Melanie! I'm so happy for you!" Gloria exclaimed. "Now, you need to nurture your self-confidence and avoid falling back into old patterns. I know that you can! Just look at how far you've come in a few weeks' time. Congratulations!"

Melanie was still beaming as Jill and Cole entered the room. Jill had a grin on her face and Cole looked very happy with himself. Melanie chirped, "What canaries did you cats swallow?"

"Have a seat," Gloria offered. "It looks like you two had some progress yourselves this week. Tell all!"

"Oh! Isn't it great about Melanie's chance at the promotion?" Jill said proudly. "I'm so glad for her! And wait 'til you hear what I did this week!"

"Out with it!" Melanie demanded.

"Well, it won't sound like much to you guys, but for me it's a real milestone!" Jill warned. "I actually fed the kids cereal for dinner one night when I'd been gone all day and was too tired to fix my usual 'banquet.' I thought they'd fall over from shock. And you know what? They were *thrilled* with my laid-back attitude. Then, Gloria, I let my son miss an assignment rather than type it for him! He wasn't too happy about that one, but he got the point of how the 'new me' is going to act!"

"Good for you, Jill!" Melanie cried. "It's about time you let those little brats fend for themselves a little!"

"Melanie!" Cole said sharply, "don't ruin a good thing!"

"Sorry, Jill," Melanie shrugged.

"No! No!" Jill shrilled. "That's the best part of my week—I'm finally able to look at my kids and see that *I'm* the one who's allowed them to become brats by doing

Because eliciting guilt and shaming family members into behavior that keeps the status quo is rampant in dysfunctional families, it usually takes members who are making progress toward restoration awhile to feel good about their newfound happiness and hope.

every little thing for them! It's so wonderful to know that I can still undo what I've done and give us all a second chance!"

Gloria smiled widely. "Jill, I'm so proud of you! You really are grasping the process of changing destructive behavior into constructive behavior! Hurray for you!"

Cole cleared his throat. He looked a little sheepish and then said quietly, "I had an all-right week too. I ignored Shel's negative behavior almost the whole time! Just flat out ignored it and went on with my business!"

"And how did that make you feel?" Gloria asked.

"Well," Cole answered, "good and guilty—at the same time."

"Very usual," Gloria nodded. "It takes awhile to get used to new behaviors. When you begin to see more and more positive rewards of change, you'll pick up momentum to carry you further on the road to restoration. I can't tell you how proud and full of gratitude I am for the three of you! You are truly in the midst of reconciliation."

As Gloria finished her sentence, Rod, Mike and Nora walked into the office. Gloria breathed a silent thanks and stood to greet them. She extended her hand to Mike and smiled warmly. "I'm so glad to see you again."

"Yeah, well, I guess a couple more times won't hurt anything," Mike remarked.

"Everyone take a seat," Gloria directed. "Let's get going. Rod, your brother and sisters have reported some fine happenings in their lives this week as they applied the techniques to implement change that we discussed at our last session. Do you have anything to share?"

Rod looked at Gloria with slightly glazed eyes. Gloria wondered what was going on with this young man. He said simply, "Nope. All's the same with me."

Melanie, Cole and Jill shifted uncomfortably in their

places. Gloria recognized the uneasiness as probable guilt over their having good news while their brother still wallowed in his misery. After all, life is "supposed" to stay the same in order for the old network to remain bonded. Because eliciting guilt and shaming family members into behavior that keeps the status quo is rampant in dysfunctional families, it usually takes members who are making progress toward restoration awhile to feel good about their newfound happiness and hope. Gloria treated Rod's response with indifference instead of the usual pity and over-concern he was probably used to getting from family members.

Gloria asked the group, "Last week, I asked you to think about who you are now and who you wanted to become if the two are different. Melanie, will you start by telling me who you are?"

"Sure." Melanie's victorious mood was not to be broken by Rod's defeatist attitude. "I'm a career woman on her way to success!"

"And is that who you want to be?" Gloria asked seriously.

"Yep!" Melanie spoke quickly.

"Anything else?"

"Um—" Melanie put an index finger on her chin. "I guess I'd like to add a few things as I go—like a husband and children, and to be well-grounded inside."

"Anything else?"

"Well, should there be?" Melanie asked.

"Not necessarily," said Gloria. "There really aren't any shoulds or shouldn'ts to a question like 'Who are you?' It's a matter of how you view yourself as a total person. For instance, do you see yourself exclusively as someone else's wife, daughter or mother? Do you see yourself as a person whose worth is attached only to the kind of career you're in? These kinds of things can indicate areas of your life to work on."

"Like me!" Jill interrupted. "I've always looked at myself as someone's mom or wife or worker—never just Jill!"

"Okay, Jill." Gloria went with the flow. "Tell me how you feel right now about who you are."

"I feel like a light is starting to come on in my brain. I'm beginning to believe it's okay to find out just who I am as a separate woman—a person—and not always to be a Siamese twin to someone or something else! I know the ingredients are there, because I'm loving and caring and I have lots of things that I can remember—small bits of what I used to want to do for myself before I got tied into a miserable marriage and my perfectionist merry-go-round. But I can't really answer who I am right now. I'd like to become someone who's content, happy and creative—a woman who is at peace with herself and who sparkles from the inside out."

"Tall order," Rod said sourly.

Gloria turned to him. "Why does it irritate you that Jill has such admirable goals?"

"It doesn't irritate me—it makes me sad for her that she's so unrealistic!" answered Rod.

"And why do you think it's unrealistic?" Gloria questioned.

"Aw, here we go again with the third degree! Can't you just leave me alone?" Rod shot back.

"I'm only asking to provoke your thoughts, Rod," Gloria assured him. "You may be surprised to find that there's no real reason for some of your pessimism."

"Pessimism!" Rod was incredulous. "Ha! Down to earth is more like it! These guys sit here staring at their own navels and everyone else's. For what? For nothing!

So we grew up in a family that wasn't perfect! Big deal! No one has a perfect family. We take the cards we're dealt and play with 'em!"

"Essentially, you think that your being in an alcoholic family is just the bad luck of the draw then?" asked Gloria.

"I didn't say bad," Rod responded quickly. "I just think these turkeys are wasting their time pretending they can make their lives perfect—it's just not in the cards for them!"

"So, trying to better yourself, make yourself happier or more fulfilled is a waste of time to you?" Gloria prodded.

"Look, I have a right to my opinions and I don't like you picking them apart all the time! And I have a right to feel that way!"

"You certainly do, Rod," Gloria agreed. "Will you tell me, then, who you see yourself as?"

"Okay, okay," Rod shrugged. "You'll poke at me until I tell anyway so I'll just get it over with! I'm Rod—a young guy, kinda ornery, a goof-off and a writer. Period. No more. No less."

Gloria surprised Rod by accepting what he said without further question. She turned to Cole. "How about you, Cole? Who are you?"

"Let's see," Cole looked like he was thinking hard. "I'm Cole, Shel's husband, Mike and Nora's son, and a teacher. I'd like to add to this list, but I really don't know how."

"Okay," Gloria smiled, "let's see what we've found out here—I'll tell you who I am and you see how you might fit your own selves into the overall picture of who you want to become. I'm Gloria. I am a child of God. I am a woman, citizen, wife, mother, sister, daughter, granddaughter, counselor, errand girl, bookkeeper, caregiver, teacher, cook, laundress, maid, social secretary and whatever else I choose to be on any given day. I'm warm, caring, creative, attractive, intelligent, thoughtful, loving, sensitive, peaceful, joyful, happy and successful. I get sad, frustrated, angry, disappointed, hurt and grieved at times. I try never to stop growing, changing and becoming the kind of person that God's calling me to be at any particular time of my life.

"Does that sound like an answer to who I am?"

"It sounds like you're your own biggest fan!" Rod said sarcastically.

"Maybe to you," Gloria acknowledged. "But there's nothing wrong with loving yourself. Things like conceit, arrogance and self-righteousness come when you use who you are to control, hurt, manipulate or abuse others. As long as I keep my priorities straight, then I am free to be just who God created me to be with no shame or insecurities. Genesis 1:27 says, 'God created man in his own image, in the image of God he created him; male and female he created them.' I am made in God's image! So are each of you! Of course, we're all human and can't begin to reach perfection! However, God anticipated this, and He sent His Son to earth to live a human life, die a human death and be resurrected in a *super*human way so we could *all* be reconciled to God through Him, just as 2 Corinthians 5:17-19 tells us!

"I experienced this reconciliation in my life several years ago. You see, I am a recovered alcoholic. I have been sober for more than 20 years now. But my alcoholism cost me a marriage and the custody of two children."

The Martin family stared at Gloria. Not one of them would have guessed that Gloria related to their problems so intimately.

Melanie expressed what they were all feeling. "Wow! I

can't believe it—you seem so—so—normal!"

Gloria laughed. "Of course I'm normal. We're all normal in our own, struggling ways."

"Why didn't you tell us this before?" demanded Mike.

"Because it would not have meant what it does now that you know me better. You've seen me work with you through some of your most private feelings. Now you are beginning to see that it really is possible for us all to work through our problems and become stronger, more complete people. That's what reconciliation and restoration are all about—changing our destructive patterns into constructive ones and becoming the healed people God wants us to be!

"You know, we pick up stereotypes of who we think alcoholics are, or who their children, parents and other associates are. Then we see someone who doesn't fit our stereotyped ideas and it blows our images apart. My parents were not alcoholics. I didn't physically abuse anyone. I wasn't physically abused. I kept a job, took care of my home and raised my children while I was drinking.

"But my husband couldn't live with my alcoholism. He walked out on me. Then I fell apart. I drank more and more until I couldn't keep up even the appearance of having it all together. My husband filed for divorce and got custody of our two children. I hit rock bottom about a year after that. There were very few formal programs to help alcoholics back then, so to get sober I went to the Midwest, where one of the first treatment centers in the country was located. It was hard—*very hard*—but sometimes the hardest things to do are the best for us.

"A few years later I met and married my second husband. We have two children who are teenagers now. And, as you can see, I finished my education and got a degree in counseling."

"When did you become a Christian?" Nora asked quietly.

"Not until after I married my second husband. He became a Christian before me. He never pushed his beliefs on me or tried to force me to accept Christianity. As I got healthier, I was still missing something in my life. I had my marriage and a new baby, my career was getting established, but I still felt the need of something more.

"One night when I had the flu and couldn't sleep, I got up and went into the living room and sat in a rocking chair. My husband's Bible was on an end table and I picked it up and flipped through the pages. It fell open to John 14:6— 'Jesus answered, "I am the way and the truth and the life. No one comes to the Father except through me."' I decided that I wanted to get to know Jesus. And my life has been a wonderful adventure ever since! It hasn't been all fun and happy, of course, but even through the toughest moments I've had more security than in my best times before I became a Christian."

The Martin family sat with quiet respect for several seconds before Nora said softly, "I think that's wonderful for you, Gloria. I almost feel ashamed that I was uncomfortable having you know our family problems."

"Thank you, Nora, I appreciate your support. But you needn't be ashamed—most of us would prefer to keep our weaknesses and faults out of sight. I don't think very many people are comfortable exposing their vulnerability. But I think that, as we have the courage to expose our extremely human needs—and we all *do* have our own problems and skeletons—we give others the courage to do the same. And the more of ourselves we expose, the more we find that others share our pain and heartbreak. We realize that we're not inferior because we have troubles and imperfections—rather, we're stronger and closer to making ourselves the best we can be by reaching out to others through our weaknesses.

"In fact, Nora, I'd like to talk more about the issues you said were bothering you at the session before last." Gloria looked at her notes. "You expressed a feeling of humiliation that the family's problems were publicly exposed through our counseling sessions. More importantly, you expressed some resentment at Mike for being the cause of all the upheaval because he got picked up while drunk and, as a result, you all had to have family counseling. You also felt like you live with depression and fatigue, possibly a result of filling your life too full with activities because of the demands of a stressful family life. Have I interpreted what you said correctly?"

"Uh-huh," Nora nodded hesitantly. Gloria saw her steal a look at Mike.

"Let me ask you, Nora—do you experience a lot of physical illnesses or aches and pains of different kinds?"

"Oh, I don't know," Nora thought out loud. "I guess you could say I usually catch whatever bug's in the air for the season. I have some migraine headaches every so often and I have quite a bit of heartburn. But that's all."

"Mom!" Melanie piped up, "I can't remember a time when I've asked you how you feel and you just said, 'Great!'—you always have something that's a little bit wrong, even if it's a tiny hangnail or scratch somewhere!"

Gloria looked at Nora and asked, "How does that make you feel?"

Nora bit at the inside of her cheek and considered before she answered. "A little bit defensive. But then I have to be honest—Melanie's probably right. I really *don't* ever feel just great, and I don't know why—I'm never seriously sick or anything."

"Let me give you a little food for thought," Gloria suggested. "People who live under a great deal of stress for long periods of time often develop stress-related physical symptoms. Headaches, stomachaches, diarrhea, constipation, painful muscle spasms, heartburn, joint pains and a host of other symptoms can be stress related. That's not to say that they always are—anything that is unusual or lasts for several days in a row should be checked out with your medical doctor. But it is generally recognized that severe stress which isn't released or managed can prompt everything from suppression of the immune system to heart attacks. Stress is nothing to take lightly, especially in today's world! Find out all you can about stress-related diseases and reactions, and then find a stress management program that fits your particular life-style.

"Since I spend a lot of time in emotionally intense situations and work with people under stress, I follow a plan to make sure the stress doesn't get to *me*! My general plan can be varied to work for anyone:

"One, eat a sensible diet that includes all of the food groups.

"Two, get regular exercise and try to vary the type—I may walk one or two evenings a week, bicycle on Saturdays, swim at the YMCA one noon hour, and do calisthenics a couple of times per week also. Some people take aerobics classes, lift weights, play racquet games, or do any number of other healthy physical activities. The key to effective exercise is to do what you enjoy.

"Three, take care to get plenty of good, restful sleep. Try not to depend on medications to help you sleep. Rather, look into natural aids, such as the good ol' mug of warm milk at bedtime.

"Four, I make it a point to do something just for me once a week—I may take an extra long bubble bath or go to lunch alone. Other ideas might be to get a massage, lay

in a hammock and read, window shop, fly a kite, sip a leisurely cup of herb tea on the patio, or whatever else
makes you feel good about being your own company.

"Five, I find that I can release a lot of tension and keep
stress in perspective by spending regular time with loved
ones and friends. Talking to others—voicing what's going
on in your life and your head—can really be a stress
reducer. By putting feelings and thoughts into words, we
can often desensitize ourselves to extreme pressures we
may be experiencing. My husband and I go out for a nice
dinner together at least once a month. I try to lunch with
my husband and good friends often. I still go to AA meetings periodically to keep myself grounded and thoughtful.

"Six, I pray a lot. Throughout my day, I talk with God.
I may simply tell Him, 'Lord, you know this problem is
really weighing on my mind. Please help me to give it up to
you and be rid of it myself!' Sometimes I sing hymns in the
shower.

"Prayer is our direct communication link to God. It is
powerful and necessary for our well-being. Jesus assured
us in Matthew 6:8, 'Your Father knows what you need
before you ask him.' Often, we don't really allow Him into
our daily lives. We're afraid God will think we're weak if
we ask Him to help us meet our obligations, or that He
won't have time to help us release our stress. But Jesus
said in John 14:14, 'You may ask me for anything in my
name, and I will do it.'

"The really wicked thing about stress is that it can
pounce and suddenly show its symptoms without our even
knowing it's been working on us for months or years. We
may think we really have things under control, and all of a
sudden they start to crunch and clash.

"One of my clients turned up with gynecological problems at a routine exam. She couldn't understand why—

she'd never had trouble before. However, her doctor knew her well and pointed out that she and her husband had been having marital problems for many months, they'd filed bankruptcy the year before and had been under tremendous financial strain, and their oldest son had graduated from high school and gone off to college. Her doctor felt that the severe stressors that had been plaguing her manifested themselves in physical problems.

"Another client found out he was grinding his teeth in his sleep and had thrown his jaw out of place, which in turn caused several other physical problems. He'd been bothered by personal problems that couldn't surface during the day because he was 'too busy' to take care of himself. So the problems surfaced at night when he wasn't so resistant.

"We need positive stress to motivate us—if we feel healthy pressure we tend to get off our fannies and *move*—but we must manage our stress instead of letting it manage us. Stress demands release in one form or another—why not let it out regularly in constructive ways instead of allowing it to burst out when we least want or expect it to?

"In your case, Nora, how might your physical symptoms be related to stress?"

Nora was taken aback by Gloria's abrupt question. She answered honestly before she had time to think her answer through. "Why, putting up with Mike's drinking and all the family problems, of course!"

All eyes turned to Nora. No one looked more shocked than she did herself. Nora turned white and put a hand over her mouth as if to check if she was really the one who had made the exclamation.

"Now you've done it!" Rod exploded at Gloria. "You've tricked Mom into saying what you wanted her to say all along, didn't you?"

"Hush, Rod," Nora told him. "Sometimes the truth just comes out when we let our guards down a little, I guess."

"That's right, Nora," Gloria said gently. "It's nothing to be ashamed of. It's high time you paid more attention to your own needs and took care of some of the stress that's been on you for such a long time. Then you can gain your full strength and health back."

Mike cleared his throat. Rod slumped down in his chair angrily. Jill, Cole and Melanie sat in rigid silence, waiting for what might happen next. Nora seemed to shrink into the back of the love seat. Gloria let the moment sink in before she turned to Mike.

"Mike, I'd like you to tell me how you feel about what Nora just said."

Mike stared down at his hands in his lap. He raised his head slowly and met Gloria's gaze straight on. "It makes me feel like a complete ass! I think it's just too hard to face all the damage I've done to this family and I just want to disappear from the face of the earth—but you know, I'm too d– – – chicken even to do them that much of a favor. I make them miserable living around them, but I just can't—" Mike's voice broke.

"Can't what, Mike?" Gloria asked compassionately.

"Can't live without them!" Mike sobbed. "I know it's the booze! I try to stay away from it. But I keep going back to it! Over and over and over! Every time I do I feel more ashamed and guilty. I just don't know how to stop it!"

Gloria looked at the tears streaming down Mike's face. Even after all these years, it still wrenched her heart afresh each time she saw a family in the midst of all the pain and heartbreak that alcoholism brings. She referred to her notes from the last time Mike had shared his feelings and spoke quietly. "You know, shame and guilt are prominent in your life. Last time you were here you told me that you have too much pride, that you are bitter and lonely and that you're a failure. Are those issues still up front in your mind?"

Mike nodded as he wiped the back of his hands across his eyes. Instead of all his family members gathering around him, like they had the last time he wept, they sat with mixtures of pain and compassion on their faces. Nora leaned forward and grabbed a tissue from a box on the coffee table. She handed it to Mike and let her hand fall to rest on his shoulders.

Gloria asked, "Mike, can you tell us about your destructive behavior? Maybe if you explain to your family how it is for you, it might help *all* of you to finish the reconciliation process and get on to more construction relationships within the family and out in the world."

"I don't know," Mike said jerkily, "it's just like I'm on automatic pilot—I promise myself I'll never drink again after every night I've been out. Then, something happens that makes me want to relax, and next thing I know, I'm at the tavern or in the liquor cabinet. If I have a fight with Nora or one of the kids, I usually get drunk afterwards. I guess I just get tired of all the petty junk that goes on! I still say I wouldn't drink if I didn't have so much on my mind all the time! I need a couple of belts to unwind."

Despite his rationalization, Mike's misery and fear were very plain to Gloria. She asked, "How do you view your family with relation to your drinking?"

"No question—" Mike blurted, "as interference! They interfere with my drinking! They're always on my back, wanting me to do this or not do that! If they'd mind their own business I'd be fine!"

Gloria was quiet for a moment. Then she asked, "And how does God fit into the picture?"

"Well, of course He won't accept me—not while I'm still drinking!" Mike exclaimed. "I can't very well expect Him to take care of me when I keep breaking promises to *myself*!"

"I'm hearing you say that you're lonely, Mike." Gloria left the issue of God for the time being. "Is that correct?"

Mike dissolved into tears as a small child might. "Yes! Yes! I'm so lonely I don't know what to do!"

"And so you drink to escape the loneliness?" Gloria asked.

Mike nodded his head and gulped, "Yeah—I look at a bottle and know that relief's just a swallow away."

"Why do you think you're so lonely?"

"Like I said before—because no one really understands me, and so they can't help me stay sober. I mean, it's not like I take the first drink and intend to get blitzed or hurt someone! I can be sitting at home watching TV and not have any intention of going out or drinking. Then one of those beer commercials will come on. I'll watch the people—all smiling and having fun—and see the little drops of ice-cold water on the can and all of a sudden I can smell the bar, hear the glasses clinking and that's it—I'm off and running!"

"Do you think it's your family's responsibility to understand you and help you stay sober?"

"Yes! Well, no!" Mike looked confused. "Yes and no. I don't expect them to be able to make me stop drinking or take the problem away. But if they would just look deeper into how I'm feeling and the awful pain I'm going through! Sometimes I sit in the bar and watch the clock—petrified that the bar's gonna close and I'm going to have to go home. I dread going home and seeing the disgust or disappointment on Nora's face!"

"That's it!" howled Rod. "What about the pain you

cause us? Huh? We're supposed to understand why *you* act. like a total jerk and feel sorry for *you*, but you don't have to be accountable to us at all? Give me a break!"

"I never said that, Rod!" Mike yelped. "I just want somebody to try to understand what I go through! I live in this vicious, rotten circle and I feel like there's no way out! When I do go home after drinking, I pass out. As soon as the first ray of light hits my brain the next morning I know I messed up. Then I have to spend the rest of the day cleaning up from the night before."

"Hold up." Gloria lifted a hand in Rod's direction as he leaned forward in his chair to speak. "You said you 'have to clean up from the night before,' Mike. Please explain what you mean by that."

"Well, I know what buttons to push to get back in everyone's good graces. Like this—I know Nora loves to go shopping and I hate it. So after I've been out drinking, maybe I'll offer to take her to the mall. That way I feel like I've done something extra to show her I'm sorry."

"It sounds like you spend a lot of time and energy manipulating others, drinking, and then making up for any trouble you've caused," Gloria said.

"Hmpf!" Mike grunted. "Just like I said at first—a total ass! My life's slipping away from me right under my very own nose and I can't do anything about it. Now my kids are a third of the way through their lives and they have to deal with all this muck on top of everything else. And Nora— I—uh—" Mike choked up again.

"Nora what?" Gloria urged him to finish.

"Nora's had this whole load to carry on her back for so long!" Mike wailed. "I don't mean to hurt her but I just can't stop! I keep thinking Nora and the kids should be good enough reasons to stop my drinking, but they're just not! I'm actually paying good money for all this destruction and misery too! And Nora's had to sacrifice because of all the money I've spent! Why aren't these things reasons enough for me to stop?"

The pleading in Mike's voice was genuine. Gloria looked him square in the eyes and said, "I suspect it's because instead of facing the challenge of breaking your addiction, you're running from it. You must be honest with yourself, Mike. You must be able to say to yourself that you are an alcoholic. For you, there is no harmless or social drinking. Every drink is potentially lethal. You must love *yourself* enough to want to stop drinking. Nora and the kids are important to you. But you're addicted to a powerful drug, Mike, and an addict is always selfish in destructive ways. Right now you are too selfish to stop drinking just for your wife's or children's sakes. You must want to stop for your own sake.

"One of my clients who's sober says she stopped drinking when she went through a transformation of attitude—like changing the floppy disk program on a computer, she had to change her attitude disk. When she saw her addiction from a completely different perspective she was able to say, 'I need to quit for my sake and the others in my life will benefit from that naturally.' Once you can face the fact that you really must quit you have a foundation to stand on. Then the struggle becomes a matter of finding ways to not fall off that foundation. This is a huge part of the reconciliation stage of your recovery."

"Ha!" Rod butted in. "Reconciliation? He's still back at the identification stage!"

"You should talk, Rod!" Melanie countered. "You're so cruel! Daddy's trying to be open and tell us how he feels, and you have to be so sarcastic! Why don't you just go crawl in a cave somewhere and feel sorry for yourself all alone?"

"Oh, Melanie, shut up!" Rod hollered. "You don't know one thing about how I feel!"

"Well, it's not like we haven't given you a chance to tell us," Jill said. "Rod, it's not fair for you to just sit there and sabotage everything that the rest of us say. Life's not just going to open up before you so you can walk down some rose-lined path. You need to jump in here with the rest of us and really get involved."

"Who asked you?" Rod demanded. "Just leave me alone!"

Gloria waited several seconds to see if the exchange was going to lead anywhere. No one said anything more so she spoke. "Well, I think we've had a full load of counseling tonight. Some vital things are out in the open and we've gotten a clearer picture of what reconciliation's all about. Mike, your sharing will hopefully lead you into some discoveries about what you can do to work toward sobriety. Changing the destructive patterns into constructive ones is the thing to remember!

"Next week at this time, go to the cafeteria down the hall from this office. And please bring blank notebooks and pens with you. Your last session will start with a talk I'm giving for all my clients who've been in counseling. I'll be speaking on the restoration process. Afterwards, I want you six to come back here with me to wind things up. Of course, if you want to continue counseling as a group or individually, I'll be happy to talk about that with you.

"Over the next several days, think more about your own personalities and life-styles. Try to come to next week's session with an optimistic, open mind. Pray this week for help in working through your problems and looking forward to a healthy future.

"Mike, please consider this: You seem to feel that God can't or won't accept you as long as you're still drinking, but in Luke 19:10 Jesus says, 'The Son of Man came to seek and to save what was lost.' You know, if God only accepted the righteous, no one would be saved. You're no exception, Mike. God knows your struggles and wants to help you all the more because of them. Pick up your Bible this week and read about the prodigal son in Luke 15:11-32 and the lost sheep in Matthew 18:10-14."

The Martin family left that evening with plenty on their minds to mull over. Gloria hoped her talk next week would lighten their loads by giving them specific things they could do to work through restoration—the final stage in the process of recovery.

Exercise Seven

Changing Destructive Patterns into Constructive Ones in Relationships

You may have grown up believing that, above all else, you should do whatever has to be done to keep harmony in relationships. Of course, this is a double standard if you are a member of an alcoholic family network. It may have been fine for Dad or Mom to scream their heads off at each other and at the kids or to pass out stone cold in a chair after dinner—as long as *you* didn't interfere and cause any waves!

As an adult, you may be prone to doing only the things that other family members want to do, in order to keep the peace—even if these are things you hate. It's your "duty" to do things you don't like as long as others are enjoying themselves—right?

Wrong! In a healthy family, compromise is the name of the game. No one member is all "taker" or all "giver"— each person takes turns at giving and receiving. Remember: *You can't truly love others and give to them unless you are centered yourself!*

Build on the things that family members have in common, and downplay differences. For example, do things together that most of you like, and give each other freedom to do your own things alone or with friends.

What to Do

Write the names of members of your immediate family across the top of a sheet of paper. (Or, write the names of friends and others with whom you have significant relationships.) Include yourself.

Under each name, list every thing you can think of that that person likes. List activities (water skiing), areas of interest (art) and even things like sleeping in on Saturdays!

When you get done, compare your lists. Then make a master list of the things your family or you and your friends enjoy in common.

You may discover that you have more common interests than you thought! If there aren't many specifics, but several things you all enjoy in general, build on these. If the kids love to scuba dive and you like to read, sit on the beach with a book while they dive. If you and your spouse like to go out to eat and the kids like to go to the movies, combine an evening as a family by doing both.

There are many ways to combine interests if all are willing to compromise! Take the time and make the effort to get to know each other. Take turns. Respect each other's differences. *Love yourself enough to love others*!

Stage 5

RESTORATION

Risking the adventure of finding your unique personality
blueprint—and happiness, inner peace, joy and life!

Finding Your Personality Blueprint

From behind her podium, Gloria surveyed the group of about 25 seated people. No matter how many times she spoke on the alcoholic family network, she still got nervous before starting a session. She still remembered the feelings of more than 20 years ago when she was nervous over something and relieved her own tension by pouring a large vodka and lime over ice. She knew the sufferings and agonies of the people who were looking to her for leadership today.

Her audience was made up of broken people trying to glue themselves back together and become stronger and healthier. There in the front row was David Miller, whose wife had run off while on a drinking binge, leaving him to care for three little children. There was Elizabeth Rosetti, whose son was in jail, convicted of manslaughter after he'd killed a young mother and her baby in an auto accident while he was driving drunk. There were the Harris twins, with two alcoholics for parents and a host of personal problems that stemmed from growing up in a home traumatized by alcohol, sexual abuse and mental cruelty.

The Martin family was in her audience tonight. All six were there, seated together. Gloria breathed a silent prayer for God's guidance in what she was about to say to these people.

"Good evening," Gloria began. "You all know me as Gloria, your counselor. Most of you also know that I'm a recovered alcoholic. I'd like to talk to you tonight about being an alcoholic and a member of an alcoholic family network. The roots in an alcoholic family can grow very deep and very tangled, as you well know.

"For those of you who drink, let me tell you this: when I stopped drinking I noticed immediate benefits in my life—I was more ambitious, my energy level was higher, I was more clear-headed, and had better self-control.

"I also had to face the realities of what alcoholism had done to my life. I had to confront the fact that I'd ruined my marriage and lost two beautiful children. I still live with the latter consequence today. Although those children are now young adults, they have problems trying to establish a healthy relationship with me. They harbor resentment, bitterness and anger toward me. I look at my other two healthy teenagers from my happy second marriage and I mourn the lost opportunity to parent, and grieve over the pain I caused the two older ones. My first husband still hasn't completely gotten over the tragic break-up of our family and has feelings of hostility over the fact that, when I put my life back together, he was left to deal with the pieces from the old days. These are things I must live with. The people who are close to me must also live with them in one way or another. Recovery hasn't been completely a rosy picture, by any means. It won't be for you, either.

"But through the Lord's infinite love and wisdom, I have found ways to turn my weaknesses into strengths. I have found that, by being needy myself, I can meet other people's needs. Second Corinthians 5:17 says, 'If anyone is in Christ, he is a new creation; the old has gone, the new has come.' Those words certainly have been proven true in my life!

"For those of you who aren't alcoholic and have lived with the pain your alcoholic spouse, parent or child has brought into your life, I want to stress three things:

"One, you cannot help the alcoholic in your life—or anyone else, for that matter—unless that person wants help!

"Two, you *do not* have to tolerate abusive behavior from others!

"Three, you are not responsible for the alcoholic's behavior!

"If you are an alcoholic and you want to get or stay sober, here are a few ways to do so. Your family and loved ones may take opportunities they see to help you adhere to some of the things in this outline. But do not, and I repeat, *do not* think that it is your loved ones' responsibility to make things easier for you. They may be so fed up with the problems you've caused that they just can't bring themselves to trust your new sobriety, or they may simply have given up hope that life will get any better in your family. An alcoholic must take total responsibility for his or her happiness! Your loved ones should not feel guilty over any feelings of indifference or intolerance they have toward you right now.

"As time rolls by and the members of your family network advance in the restoration process, there will be a natural processing of emotions. One day, you may be able to honestly say that you've fully recovered from your ordeal. Forgiveness, compassion, love, trust and hope may be fully restored in your family. But each person must take action toward his or her own health and joy as if the family may never be united in full recovery."

Gloria breathed deeply. Her audience was attentive. She never knew how much of what she said might sink in. Even a few years down the road, one of these people might be in circumstances that prompted him or her to remember a phrase or experience she told tonight.

Gloria went on. "The first, and perhaps most important thing for alcoholics to do in order to get and stay sober is this: Become familiar with the Twelve-Step Recovery Program of Alcoholics Anonymous!" Gloria outlined the steps as they appeared in her notes.

We:

1. Admitted we were powerless over alcohol—that our lives had become unmanageable.

2. Came to believe that a Power greater than ourselves could restore us to sanity.

3. Made a decision to turn our wills and our lives over to the care of God as we understood Him.

4. Made a searching and fearless moral inventory of ourselves.

5. Admitted to God, to ourselves, and to another human being the exact nature of our wrongs.

6. Were entirely ready to have God remove all these defects of character.

7. Humbly asked Him to remove our shortcomings.

8. Made a list of all persons we had harmed, and became willing to make amends to them all.

9. Made direct amends to such people wherever

possible, except when to do so would injure them or others.

10. Continued to take personal inventory and when we were wrong promptly admitted it.

11. Sought through prayer and meditation to improve our conscious contact with God as we understood Him, praying only for knowledge of His will for us and the power to carry that out.

12. Having had a spiritual awakening as the result of those steps, we tried to carry this message to alcoholics and to practice these principles in all our affairs. [1]

Gloria paused, took a deep breath and continued. "Here are some other suggestions that may help you or a loved one to stay sober:

"One, *keep constructively busy*! Set goals and find incentives to make life worthwhile. A bored, idle mind is open to all sorts of negative influence.

"Two, *stay away from situations that tempt you to drink*. Usually, this means cutting all ties with alcohol—especially the drinking environment and drinking pals. Whatever works for you is what's best! You will probably need to find a new, healthy network of friends. Fellow alcoholics (unless they are all sober) are not a good support system.

"Three, *program yourself to call or go see a friend, a loved one, or* **anyone** *who can listen to you and help you stay sober*. Especially if you see the old signposts in front of you along the way to taking that first drink—go talk to anybody about *anything* to give yourself time to build up resistance!

"Four, *do something physical instead of drinking*. Each time you get the urge to drink, take a long walk, go for a swim, lift weights, dance, or do anything else that will divert your attention and help build you up instead of tear you down.

"Five, *change habits of self-focusing.* When you want to drink, when you feel self-pity or hopelessness, reach outside yourself and make a connection with someone else. Do something nice for someone— even a stranger—instead of drinking and hurting others. Go sit on a park bench or near a playground. Pushing a child on a swing or wiping a scraped knee can fill you up inside and keep selfishness under control. It can be a tremendous blessing to give to others instead of taking away from them.

"Six, *save in a jar the money you usually spent drinking.* Watch the jar fill. Set a date to count it and decide what you want to spend it on as a reward for your sobriety. You can buy yourself something you've wanted, pay for a weekend away with a loved one, buy gifts for your family, deposit the money into a savings account and save for a bigger goal.

"Seven, *get in the habit of calling on the Lord when you are tempted.* First Corinthians 10:13 says, 'No temptation has seized you except what is common to man. And God is faithful; he will not let you be tempted beyond what you can bear. But when you are tempted, he will also provide a way out so that you can stand up under it.'

"Eight, *don't be afraid of the new person you will become.* Some people stay with old habits, no matter how destructive they are, simply out of fear of the unknown. Don't worry—you're not giving up or wasting all your previous life. God will take the experiences you've had and the person you are and blend them into

God will take the experiences you've had and the person you are and blend them into something better than you ever thought possible!

something better than you ever thought possible! Remember that Romans 8:28 says, 'And we know that in all things God works for the good of those who love him, who have been called according to his purpose.'

"This can be extremely difficult for members of the alcoholic family network to believe—both that 'in all things God works for the good of those who love Him' *and* that He has called them for a purpose. Believe that it's true—all the pain, stress, humiliation, anguish and torment you've gone through *can* be transformed into effective and powerful tools so you can enjoy the best that life can give!

"Look at the time from now on as an opportunity to heal, progress, restore, recover and overcome! Take this chance to begin mending fences and knitting your families and personal lives back together again. It's a great life—if you'll spend the time and love yourselves enough to take control of it.

"For those of you who are not alcoholics: support your drinking family members as best you can as they try to get sober. If your own feelings are too negative to contribute anything positive, then try not to interfere or show open hostility toward them as they struggle to get a handle on their lives.

"Now, for *all* of you: the restoration process can be an exciting experience—one you may never have thought possible! Let me describe this process for you.

"In healthy families, the inner needs of each family member are respected and hopefully met, and natural abilities and interests are fostered. As a member of an alcoholic or otherwise dysfunctional family, *your* inner needs and abilities were most likely squelched.

"Over the years, this emotional abuse has a snowballing effect, dragging you further and further away from the nuclear personality you were born with. As an adult, you may feel a persistent sense of frustration without really knowing why.

"Here's the good news: You still have the personality blueprint of that small child deep within you. You can free that child from the restrictions placed on his or her abilities and yearnings. You can nurture that child's growth and free yourself from the baggage of the past.

"Only when we are free from that baggage are we free to appreciate ourselves. In order to be whole as adults, we must know where we've been and where we want to go; by seeking and nurturing the inner child, we can redirect where we're going.

"As you work through restoration to full recovery, you may be pleasantly surprised by a metamorphosis in how you see yourself and others in your life. You may even discover that you can be completely liberated from the effects of growing up with alcoholism or other traumas. You have absolutely nothing to lose and everything to gain—take this opportunity to feel the great burdens that you carry lifted from your shoulders!"

Gloria looked at the people watching her and saw a familiar glint of hope in many eyes. "Why don't we take a few minutes' break and then we'll get down to the business of searching for and finding that inner child's blueprint!"

Gloria got a cup of herb tea and left the cafeteria to spend a few quiet minutes in her office down the hall. She knew some of the people in the cafeteria would leave tonight feeling motivated and excited. Others would leave confused, and some would even feel more hopeless than when they came in. But, Gloria reflected, time has a wonderful way of stirring up things that have passed through our conscious minds and into our subconscious minds. Even the hardest cases here tonight would most likely derive some benefit from what she would say to them. Gloria drank the last of her tea and left her office.

Back in the cafeteria, she could feel anticipation in the air. She was glad. The group took their seats as she went to stand behind the podium. Gloria resumed her talk.

"God has a plan for you. As a child born into this world you had a journey ahead of you that was meant to be exciting and full. That child still exists—he or she has just been hidden for a long while. To help you begin searching for that special, loving child who lives within you, you have the words of Jesus—He wants you to live life to the fullest possible extent! He is a caring, giving Savior who wants you simply to take the key of life that He offers you.

"One reason that members of the alcoholic family network hold back is because things were rarely (if ever) simple. Following the steps I'm about to list may help you to discover more easily the blueprint God had for you when you were born.

"Please take out the blank notebooks that I asked you to bring tonight. No one else will read what you write in this notebook unless you choose to share it.

"Open the notebook to a blank page. For a moment, consider the simplicity of nothing being there. Now think of yourself as a blank page—no pain, no regrets, no demands, no expectations—you just are!

"Let the meaning of the following Scripture verses roll around in your mind: Jeremiah 1:5 says, 'Before I formed you in the womb I knew you, before you were born I set you apart'; Ephesians 2:10 says, 'We are God's workmanship, created in Christ Jesus to do good works, which God prepared in advance for us to do.'

"Look at the blank sheet of paper and *believe* that God knew you before you were born and that He set you apart. Know that He planned in advance good things for your life!

"Now, let's begin finding those good things. At the top of your first blank page, write the heading 'One Happy Memory from Childhood.' If you can't think of anything happy right now, it's okay—just bear with me. Your blueprint will begin to reveal itself as you work through the entire group of restoration exercises you'll be doing. If there aren't any good memories from your childhood, your inner child can still emerge. For now, try to think of one thing, no matter how small, that gave you pleasure when you were a youngster. You may have received a Christmas gift that was special, a hug from someone important to you, praise from a teacher; perhaps you read a book that really impressed you, or had a family pet you loved."

Gloria wrote the first heading on the chalkboard behind her, then waited silently for a few minutes while people wrote in their notebooks. Then she continued, "One way to bring back pleasant memories and feelings—and an excellent avenue to help you find your inner child—is to simply observe children. Go to parks, zoos, Little League games, the beach, a public swimming pool, or anywhere else that children gather. Watch their exuberance and zest for life! It's amazing to realize how we let the pressures of adulthood get to us and suffocate the childlike qualities that are important to well-being.

"In Matthew 18:1-3, Jesus' disciples asked Him, '"Who is the greatest in the kingdom of heaven?" He called a little child and had him stand among them. And he said: "I tell you the truth, unless you change and become like little children, you will never enter the kingdom of heaven."'

Notice, Jesus did not say that we should become child*ish*, but child*like*! In 1 Corinthians 13:11 Paul tells us, 'When I became a man, I put childish ways behind me.' The difference is that being childlike in our faith, accepting the wonders of life without pessimism, is a very desirable attribute—it is a key to heavenly places. But the destructive behavior which acts childishly over selfish, prideful things is to be put behind us. One way to rediscover childlike qualities and to be reminded of childish ways is by watching children in their favorite environments.

"Now, regardless of whether you wrote something on your happy memory list, turn to the next blank page in your notebooks. At the top of the page write 'My Ideal Day.'"

Gloria wrote this heading on the chalkboard. She turned back to the group and instructed, "Later, when you're alone, write down what your ideal day would be like. If you had all the time, money, freedom and nurturing that you wanted, how do you think you would spend a typical, ideal day? Would you laze away on a tropical island? Or be a corporate executive? Whatever you could have and do in an ideal life, on an ideal day—write it down. This description can include what you're doing alone, with personal contacts and business associates—whatever springs from within as you write it.

"Do this exercise periodically, because people don't stay the same—we grow and things change. Leave about three pages in your notebook for this exercise. When you look later at the profile of your ideal day, you will most likely see some positive childlike tendencies and desires. Pursue these to help coax your inner child to reveal itself."

Gloria turned back to the chalkboard and wrote "My Deepest Desire." She then faced the group and said, "Write this heading at the top of the next blank page in your notebook. Later, all by yourself, think of the one, deepest desire of your heart. This could be inner joy, a family, a good marriage, a fulfilling career, a home of your own—it doesn't matter. But let whatever it is come from deep inside you! Writing out this deepest desire will give you a glimpse of who your inner, original childlike self really is. He or she may be a city kid just waiting to get out of the rural area in which you live—or an artist longing for a beach residence; an athlete wanting to leave a manufacturing plant and manage a health spa; a musician wishing to break loose and perform; a self-made career person pining away for a traditional family life; or someone who is truly happy just the way he or she is, but hasn't had the skills to discover this.

"Our deepest desires are usually a reflection of who our original selves were meant to be. Hope for the *best* life has to offer!

"Hope can make the difference between a life of despair and one of joy. Proverbs 13:12 says, 'Hope deferred makes the heart sick, but a longing fulfilled is a tree of life.' Spend some time considering what would make your heart sing and your personality blossom. This search will help your inner child to surface.

"Now turn to the next blank page in your notebook and head it with what I write."

Gloria turned back to the chalkboard and wrote in rolling script, "If I Were a . . . Statements." She faced the group and smiled. "This can be a delightful exercise to help discover your inner child. Play with it. Have fun with it, be a little outrageous about it, and then study it! Here's what you do:

"Write the numbers one through ten down the side of the next pages, leaving several spaces between numbers. Beside each number write one of the following: color, tree, bird, animal, piece of furniture, article of clothing, car, toy, food, and natural resource. Now complete this statement for each item: "If I were a – – – I'd be – – – because – – –." For instance, at this point in my life, mine reads as follows:

> If I were a color, I'd be teal because it's warm and deep with happy light.
>
> If I were a tree, I'd be an oak because it's strong and respected.
>
> If I were a bird I'd be an eagle because eagles soar high above the problems of the world.
>
> If I were an animal, I'd be a tiger because they walk very softly but pack a wallop when provoked.
>
> If I were a piece of furniture, I'd be a cushy recliner because others would feel safe and comfortable with me.
>
> If I were an article of clothing, I'd be a soft, rich leather coat because they're classy.
>
> If I were a car, I'd be a luxury model because they sail over bumps in the road with hardly a notice.
>
> If I were a toy, I'd be a teddy bear because they're cuddly.
>
> If I were a food, I'd be a kiwi fruit because others are a little curious about them.
>
> If I were a natural resource, I'd be water because of its deep and endless motion.

"When you've completed all ten statements, look over your list and enjoy the 'objective' profile of the kind of person you are! That's what tends to come out when you follow your instincts about what you'd like to be! It's fun and it gives you an opportunity to experience some good, childlike play. Now you're probably getting a picture of the kinds of things that help you to find your inner child and the blueprint of the personality that God gave you before you were even born!

"You *are* worth the effort! And it's worth the effort to do our next exercise, which can also be fun and revealing! Copy this heading onto a new page in your notebook."

Gloria turned away and wrote "Flowchart" on the board. She reached beneath her podium to pull out a large piece of tagboard with a diagram on it and put the tagboard on an easel. Then she explained, "My friends, once you create a personal flowchart for any area of your life and use it, you could end up using flowcharts for many areas of your life! A flowchart is the most direct, efficient and success-producing way I know to set goals for yourself and follow them through. Since one of the problems that arises quite often in the alcoholic family network is disjointedness—a diminished ability to follow things through full circle—a flowchart can be an invaluable tool to help you get your life organized and to make your dreams reality. A flowchart can also contribute to the development of your inner child and speed up his or her emergence into your adult life.

"I've diagrammed one of my own flowcharts here. First, I'll run through the basic steps. These are always the same no matter what you're charting. Whether it's a budget, getting your housekeeping organized or plotting a course to grow a seedling company into a Fortune 500 entity, the same basic steps apply. After I run through the steps, I'll show you how I fit a personal current goal into them.

"As you can see, we start with a simple *A* which represents the point I'm at right now with anything I want to chart. Then we go to *B*, *C* and so forth, depending on how many steps it takes to realize your goal. This particular goal of mine has six steps. The last letter on a flow chart represents the point you want to reach. Whatever you want to accomplish, you can plan out your success on a flowchart like the one below because *every large success is made up of a series of smaller, sure successes.*

"This flowchart represents getting into better physical shape by swimsuit season! This may sound silly, but how many times have you said, 'I've just got to start a better exercise program!' or 'I need to start saving a little money out of each paycheck,' and then never done a thing about it? Human nature tends to let things slide when, often, all we need is a little direction.

"I'm at point *A* now—so I write underneath that I'm about eight pounds overweight and out of shape. Underneath point *F*, which I designate as six weeks from now, I write down that I want to weigh 135 pounds and be able to do 30 minutes of aerobic exercise without stopping in the middle. I know from experience that I'm not going to get to point *F* overnight. So under *B* I write that my weight will be the same, but I'll be doing ten minutes of calisthenics before my shower each morning and watching my diet. Under point *C* I write that I will have lost two pounds, I'll be eating well and doing 15 minutes of calisthenics. Under point *D*, which is my fourth week, I write that I will have lost two more pounds. I will be eating 1500 calories a day from balanced meals, and I'll be taking a 20-minute aerobic dance class. Under *E* I've noted that I'll have lost two more pounds, be continuing my diet and increasing my aerobics to 30 minutes. At point *F*, I'll have reached my goal!

A-------B-------C-------D-------E-------F--------

"It's important to remember that goals are not written in blood, and they are not to be used as a form of self-punishment or as guilt-inducers. They are guidelines to help you keep a focus on your goals and to help you monitor your progress. You may get halfway through a flowchart and see that your expectations were unrealistic. This may happen often at first, but it's a sign that your restoration process is working because you're learning to manage your time and your life better!

"Brainstorming flowcharts is a lot of fun too. If you're devising a plan to start a business, for example, and you've got your starting point and your end goal, but you're trying to figure out ways to handle the points between, write down every possible avenue to get where you want to go. List everything you think of, no matter how wild or impossible something may seem at first!

"I had a client who wanted to start her own clothing boutique. At point A she had nothing to start with except her dream idea. To own and operate a boutique was her end goal. Her flow chart was spread over two years. One of the ideas she came up with for a point in the middle was to check out the possibility of getting designer clothes for free. She told me that when she wrote it, she thought she was just wasting space on her chart. But guess what? In the end, she *did* open her boutique which was stocked for free with women's designer clothing! To fulfill another of the points on her flowchart, she talked to clothing representatives of different companies. One conversation led to another and in the end she took new, unknown designers' clothing samples into her store on consignment! I'm happy to say that this little boutique is still open today—six years later! You never know where planning, dreaming, creating and following through will carry you.

"To keep all this together during the rough times, though—the times when you're discouraged and wonder what you've gotten yourself into—you need to save a special page in your notebook. Label this page 'It's Good to Be Me!' This may sound foolish and even a little conceited, but it's not! In order to be the person that God intends you to be, you must build your self-esteem. You cannot achieve your place in God's plan if you don't love and care about yourself! When you can get up in the morning and say genuinely, 'It's good to be me!' then you've reached full recovery, having progressed from the identification of problems in your life caused by alcoholism or other dysfunctions all the way to restoration of your original personality blueprint!

"One way that I keep my self-esteem growing is to keep a list of my good character traits. When I first started the list, all I could think of to write was that I am caring. As time went on, I began to notice more positive things about myself and added them to the list. Now, when I'm blue I look them over, and usually one or two things strike a cord and give me just enough energy to get on with my day.

"Another way to develop a good feeling about yourself is to keep a record in your notebook of things that you felt positive about, one day at a time. You may have simply listened to a co-worker blow off steam or gotten through the day without a drink. Whatever the incident, list at least one positive thought for the day. During your bleaker moments, you can refer to your 'It's Good to Be Me!' list and your 'Positive Thought' journal to remind yourself that you're going to be *all right*!

"Let's review the seven steps to help you find your personality blueprint and coax out the child in you.

"One—Describe one happy memory from childhood.

"Two—Write out your ideal day.

"Three—Put your deepest desire into words.

"Four—Complete the 'If I were a . . . ' statements.

"Five—Develop flowcharts for reaching your goals.

"Six—List reasons why it's good to be you.

"Seven—Keep a 'Positive Thought' journal.

"These seven keys can help you complete the restoration stage of recovery from the effects of life in an alcoholic family network! I'm sure you can find other good suggestions in books or magazine articles to help you become the joyful person God intends you to be!

"Here's where you launch into your own adventure in finding the inner child within you.

"Take your notebooks home and fill them to overflowing. Do the exercises every so often to keep your finger on the pulse of your life's unique beat. Every second you spend on nurturing yourself is worthwhile!

"Once you've been through the full cycle of recovery for the alcoholic family network—identification, examination, recognition, reconciliation and restoration—you can safely say that you're traveling on the road of healthy adulthood!

"I want to thank you all for coming along on this journey, and I want to leave you with Numbers 6:24-26, 'The Lord bless you and keep you; the Lord make his face shine upon you and be gracious to you; the Lord turn his face toward you and give you peace.'"

Gloria drew a deep, relaxed breath. She always felt gratified when family groups had completed their eight-week counseling program.

She walked among the people getting ready to leave and assured them that if they needed further help, she'd welcome their calls. She asked the Martins to come to her office for a brief wrap-up before she signed their completion papers for Judge Harris.

As Gloria walked to her office, she wondered what would become of the Martin family. There were many areas she wished they could have explored. Gloria knew from experience that one could never exhaust all the issues in a few weeks' time. However, just covering the main bases at each stage of recovery was often all it took to send many people on their way to health. Any members of the family who wanted further help could call on her or another good counselor of their choice.

Gloria had just sat down when there was a tap on the door. Gloria answered and in came the Martins. They all sat down in the spots they were by now accustomed to. Gloria smiled at each one. They looked happy, but a little anxious as well.

Gloria asked, "What did you think of the lecture tonight?"

Jill spoke up. "I thought it was wonderful! Your suggestions are so inspiring—like taking a long walk on an autumn day!"

"Aren't you the poet!" Rod said.

Gloria shook her head. "I just don't know, Rod—I think, with that rapier-sharp tongue of yours, you ought to write a movie review column!"

Rod gave Gloria a half-smile before he realized he was on his way to a full one and stopped. He responded, "Maybe I'll do that someday."

Gloria looked around at the family. She sighed as she said, "Well, this is it, folks. I hope we've turned up enough new soil so that some good, strong roots of growth can take hold and go down deep inside each one of you! If any of you ever has any more that you'd like to discuss in counseling—together or individually—I'd certainly love to hear from you.

"Mike, I'd really like to see you go to the AA meetings in your town or here. And for the rest of you, don't hesitate to go to a support group! Those groups can be great sources of strength and comfort!

"I want you to know that I'm very proud of each one of you for coming through these eight weeks still speaking to one another and sticking it out together! I'll keep praying for you. Before you go, I want to remind you of the encouragement in Isaiah 40:31: 'Those who hope in the Lord will renew their strength. They will soar on wings like eagles; they will run and not grow weary, they will walk and not be faint.'

Gloria and Mike both signed the counseling papers required by the court. As the family began to leave, Gloria was touched by their show of affection. Mike and Cole extended their hands and said polite thank-yous. Nora, Jill and Melanie all hugged her. As Rod brought up the rear, Gloria quipped, "It's only appropriate that the first one in the door be the last one out!"

Rod patted her shoulder and said, "All I have to tell you is that it's been a real interesting experience!"

With that, they were gone. Gloria followed shortly. She was anxious to get home to her family.

Note
1. Alcoholics Anonymous (New York: Alcoholics Anonymous Publishing, Inc., 1955).

One Year Later

Gloria was looking out her office window when she saw Jill get out of her car. It had been a year since the Martin family had left counseling. Gloria hadn't heard a thing from or about them until last week when Jill had called and made an appointment to come for a private counseling session. Gloria wondered what it would reveal.

Jill walked into the room. Gloria smiled and went to give her a hug. Jill melted into smiles.

"Oh! It's so good to see you again, Gloria! You know, even though it's been a year since we've been here, I can't tell you how often the things you said and what we discussed in counseling come up in the family! It's as though you're with us every day!"

"Thank you, Jill! It's good to see you too! I think of you also! Now, to what do I owe the pleasure of your company?"

"Well, actually, I'm happy to say that I'm coming for a 'service call!' I'm getting married in a couple months and I just wanted to spend some time with you and ask you a few questions about the second time around!"

"Great! Let's have a seat over here." Gloria asked, "Do you mind if I inquire how the rest of the family is doing?"

"Not at all!" Jill replied. "I'd be hurt if you didn't. Let's see, where should I start? Daddy is still drinking. The doctor told him a few months ago that he has some condition called 'fatty liver' and that if he doesn't cut out the booze he'll probably get cirrhosis. So now Daddy's trying to quit again. Who knows? I've given up worrying about it!"

"Now, that's a healthy statement if I ever heard one!" Gloria grinned.

"You bet! I've done a lot of healthy things for myself this last year! Oh! You'll be happy to know that Mom has gotten quite a bit more independent—she doesn't take near the crud from Daddy that she used to. We're all so glad for her because she's spending time on herself—going to painting classes and ceramics and stuff like that. Daddy used to throw a fit over her doing something by herself, and then she just wouldn't go. Not any more! Now she'll stand right up to him and he doesn't know *how* to act."

Gloria laughed at the image of Nora defending her individuality and Mike's reaction of total shock. Gloria asked Jill, "And what about Cole? Are he and Shel still together?"

"Oh, yes, they're still together. In fact, Shel had a baby boy three months ago. I guess after counseling Cole must have decided to really try to make things work!" Jill giggled. "He and Shel went to counseling together for a few months after we stopped coming here. When Shel found out she was pregnant, she stopped drinking and really began to get a handle on things. We were relieved that the baby was healthy! I think Shel's been sober for at least nine months. We're all so excited for them to be together—and *happy* about it!"

"I'm so relieved to hear that!" Gloria exclaimed. "Cole really had to hang tough, but it sure seems to have been worth it!

"What about Melanie?" Gloria asked.

"She's doing fantastic! She's earned a couple of promotions this year and is dating a really great guy—he's cute and everything! She doesn't come around the folks' house much anymore—just holidays. I think she decided that she needed to stay away from the tugging and pulling of all the family problems to really break out of the mold and grow. Daddy gets mad at her, but she stands her ground and just comes on special occasions. Mom goes to visit her, but Daddy won't. He's too stubborn."

"And last, but not least, how is Rod?" Gloria asked.

"Well, Rod's another story. You know, he's the big surprise in the family to me. Just a few weeks after we finished counseling, Rod got stopped by the police for driving drunk! But that's not all—his blood test turned up other drugs too. He got wild with the officers who picked him up. They had to arrest him. He resisted. Punched one of them in the face and ended up with all sorts of charges against him! The same judge who ordered us here for counseling ordered Rod to a detox unit at our hospital! Come to find out, he's there less than 24 hours and having withdrawal symptoms! He was addicted to prescription tranquilizers! Poor kid, he's really going through it. He lost his job over that deal. He's still making payments to the hospital on the detox episode. And now he moved home with Mom and Daddy because he couldn't afford his apartment! It's just a mess."

"I'm very sorry to hear that," Gloria said sincerely. "I had hoped that Rod would work through his problems and come out all right. Is he drinking now?"

"Oh, yes! He can't get tranquilizers anymore, so he

just numbs himself with alcohol. He and Daddy make a fine pair! They'll sit down and get going on a bottle and before long they're just singing their own praises like crazy and supporting each other's views that the rest of the world has gone to hell in a handbasket!"

"Well, I'll pray for Rod and your dad, Jill. Now, tell me all about you!"

Jill beamed. "Well, I met the greatest guy in the world about a month after we left counseling. We've been dating ever since. He loves the kids and they love him and he's very well adjusted. You'd really like him, Gloria. I just wanted to check in with you for a few pointers on making this marriage forever! I can still get pretty insecure about some things and compulsive about filling my schedule up too full, but mostly I'm just so—" Jill's voice cracked and tears sprang from her eyes, "So—happy! I can't tell you how grateful I am for your guidance, Gloria!"

"I really appreciate your saying that, Jill! I don't know how much help I can give you in the marriage department, but it sounds like you're going to be fine even if I can't think of a thing to tell you!"

Of course, as they talked together, Gloria did think of several suggestions for Jill as she prepared to marry again—this time with a commitment to a man free from alcoholism, and Jill herself free from many of the problems that plagued her young adulthood. As for Jill, it was as though a door of opportunity had opened for her, and she was excited about stepping through it into a new life.

After an hour, the two friends hugged farewell. Watching at the window as Jill got in her car and drove away, Gloria recalled a passage she often thought of as she watched her clients improve: *"Here I am! I stand at the door and knock. If anyone hears my voice and opens the door, I will come in . . . . "*

The Five Stages of Full Recovery for Members of an Alcoholic Family

The first stage, *identification*, usually begins when you find yourself wondering, "What's the matter with me?" because of persistent emotional or physical problems that may not be otherwise explainable. Or perhaps you feel uncomfortable when commercials for alcohol and other drug addiction treatment centers flash across the TV screen.

As this process evolves, you begin to identify ways in which your life has been affected by alcoholism. Then the second stage, *examination*, can begin. In this stage you become like a sponge—drinking in all the information you can find on alcoholism and the ways it affects people's lives.

By examining how others react to and cope with the problems that alcoholism presents in families, you can start the third stage of recovery, *recognition*. Recognition comes when you begin realizing why you behave and feel the way you do and why you believe certain things if you have lived with alcohol-related problems. You may have to confront such painful feelings as old resentment, bitterness, anger, guilt, shame, and hatred toward your loved ones.

When you can recognize these kinds of feelings within yourself, you are well on your way to the fourth stage of recovery, *reconciliation*. Reconciliation involves forgiving yourself for any hateful, angry thoughts you may have had toward your parents, spouse, children, siblings and self. Reconciliation often involves professional counseling and/or supportive group therapy.

The issue of counseling can be a particularly sticky one for those who've lived with alcoholism. You may have been told that counseling is only for the weak. Not true! Counseling is simply a means to help you help yourself get whole. A good counselor guides you in finding your *own* way! Getting professional help is a loving, healthy thing to do for yourself and those you care about.

When you feel confident that you have confronted many of your negative feelings about your alcoholic family, you can take a very exciting step into the beginning of the fifth stage of recovery, *restoration*.

Central to the process of restoration is the conviction that God did not intend for the alcoholic(s) in your life to drink. Nor did God intend for you to experience the agony that alcoholism brings. Jeremiah 1:5 describes the personality blueprint describing God's calling for Jeremiah. And He knows each of us as intimately as Jeremiah; He has a blueprint for each of our lives. Sadly, for many in the alcoholic family network, these blueprints often get rolled up tightly and banded shut. However, they wait to be rediscovered, nurtured and developed. When you choose to embark on a journey in search of your personal blueprint, you choose life, health and fulfillment for yourself!

Like miners of precious diamonds, members of the alcoholic family network can scrape away layers of sand and dirt to find the sparkling, wondrous gems that exist within each one of us! And, like diamonds that are graded on their clarity, your level of health can be measured by honestly evaluating how clear your feelings are about other members of your family and yourself.

You may have to be very patient. Full recovery is a process—not an event! Right now you may feel like a frayed rope with problems unraveling in many areas of your life. These frayed ends need braiding back together to make you whole. Believe that you *can* reach full recovery as a happier, healthier and better person!

Today you may have many questions about problems in your life. Searching for the answers to these questions can raise emotions that you don't understand. Discussing your family's problems may cause your stomach to jump or your eyes to tear. That's okay! Physical reactions such as crying, nausea, headaches, fatigue, shaking and a rapid heartbeat are signs that you're trying to identify, confront and cope with your problems. Your emotions are coming out to make room deep inside you for healing! Try not to avoid or push your emotions—let them work their way out at a pace you can handle.

It may be frightening to feel a lump rise in your throat or have tears stream down your face unexpectedly. Let the tears flow. Bear in mind that you may have many *years* of emotions stuffed into every crevice of your mind and body—they need to come out for full recovery to take place.

On the other hand, not everyone experiences reactions such as these. You may have been "letting off steam" a little at a time for many months or years by reading, counseling, discussion with others, and introspection.

There's certainly nothing wrong with you if you don't have intense reactions as you face your family's individual problems. But there's nothing wrong with you if you do, either.

During any moment of panic you may have as you strive toward inner joy and peace, try to keep Isaiah 41:10 in your heart: "Do not fear, for I am with you; do not be dismayed, for I am your God. I will strengthen you and help you; I will uphold you with my righteous right hand."

On Survival

Regardless of the circumstances in which children of alcoholics grow up, most of them do physically survive. Emotional survival is a different matter. They often grasp for and dive into anything that they think might ease their pain and misery.

Finding a Sanctuary

Ten-year-old Joshua chose the outdoors as his escape from the tensions that riddle his family's home life. He plays in the walnut grove on the ranch where he lives. He ventures among the evergreens and often sits at the edge of the creek. Joshua delights in the gentle parts of nature and surrounds himself with its peace.

One of Joshua's favorite things to do is to play quietly near the flower beds in the late afternoon. He loves to watch the hummingbirds seek the opening blossoms and is fascinated by their wildly beating wings. Joshua is very spry. He darted a hand out one day and actually captured a hummingbird. He felt its tiny swings fluttering frantically and let it go in just a moment. Joshua was reminded of how he felt when his mother was in one of her "moods" and drinking. His heart fluttered then and he felt trapped, just as he supposed the hummingbird felt. He knew instinctively that it wasn't right to hold another living thing against its will.

Joshua automatically retreats outdoors in order to survive emotionally and to tolerate his mother's alcoholism. Other young children of alcoholics bury themselves in school, science projects, music, athletics, reading or television to cope with the gulf between what they wish life would be like and what reality is for them.

Appearances Can Be Deceiving

Around other people, the children of alcoholics may appear to be a little too extroverted. Often, these children cultivate an ability to laugh, play, talk, and otherwise participate in life with such a fervor that others simply marvel at what seems to be very well-adjusted kids.

Seem is the key word. The children of alcoholics rarely feel inside what they project outwardly. Their actions are usually a subconscious effort to hide the hurts, insecurities, guilt, confusion, shame, and despair that they battle inside. These children function under such incredible levels of anxiety and pressure that living in crisis becomes a way of life for them. Even as adults, they are often more comfortable dealing with troubled situations than peaceful times.

Adult children of alcoholics often develop what might be called the "Bartender Personality"—the ability to listen, laugh, talk, or participate socially at the right times to make things appear to be what they think is "normal."

Adult children of alcoholics often have compassion for other people's pain that is so perceptive and genuine, it makes them highly valued friends and confidants. On the other hand, they survived the emotional and/or physical abrasions of childhood by creating thick skin over their hearts; this skin may be so thick that these adults appear numb to their own feelings. Inside, however, adult children of alcoholics crave unconditional love.

Family Secrets

As small children they probably felt that there was nowhere for them to turn for help. And growing up, they learned to keep their family's life private. In verbal and nonverbal ways they were taught that Mommy or Daddy's problems were no one else's business and they (the children) sure had better not be the ones to expose any family "secrets." Even as adults, the children of alcoholism can be staunch defenders of parents who used, abused and manipulated them.

Children of alcoholic parents often take on so much responsibility, it boggles many people's minds.

Supergirl

Eleven-year-old Ashley's father, Blake, is an alcoholic. She has three younger siblings. For years, Ashley has helped her mother, Beth, with childcare, housekeeping, and appeasing Blake when he is drunk. Ashley's large, brown eyes have taken on the hollow gaze of one grown up too young. Her parents quarrel often.

One night, shortly after Beth's gallbladder surgery,

Ashley awakened to hear her father in a drunken fury shouting ugly, awful things at her mother. Blake was calling Beth vulgar names and slamming things around. Ashley crawled quietly into the hall closet and sat among the blankets so she could spring out if her mother needed help. As she peered through the louvered doors, Blake lunged at Beth, grabbed both of her arms and pushed her against a wall. He punched her in the face and threw her to the floor, yelling, "When will you learn to leave me alone, you b——?!" Finally, Blake stumbled backward and sank into a rocking chair, his head hanging toward the floor. When Ashley thought her father had calmed down enough, she emerged from the closet.

"Dad?" she ventured and Blake's head snapped up.

"What are you doing up?" he asked incredulously.

"Well, I—uh—I couldn't sleep," Ashley replied cautiously. "Dad, are you all right?"

"Yeah, baby, I'm all right," Blake said as he extended his hand to her. "Come 'ere, Ashley."

Ashley approached him slowly, not knowing if her father would remain calm or fly off into another rage. But he bundled her onto his lap and hugged her tight. She breathed a momentary sigh of relief. She knew her father. When he reached this stage of drunkenness, he would soon be ready to go to his bed and pass out until the next day.

"Oh, baby," Blake crooned softly as he rocked his daughter, "I don't know what's wrong with me! Your mom makes me so mad sometimes. I don't mean to hurt her! I love her!"

"Dad," Ashley asked suddenly, "are you and Mom going to get a divorce?"

"No! No, sweetheart," Blake assured her. "We'll be fine. We won't get a divorce!" Blake rocked the chair a few more minutes in silence until his head began to nod. "I better get to bed," he said.

"Okay, Dad," Ashley said, not knowing if she was glad or sorry that her parents weren't going to get a divorce. "I'll tuck you in."

When Blake was in bed and snoring, Ashley felt safe to go to her mother. Beth was shivering in a heap on the floor. Ashley knelt down and whispered, "Come on, Mom, let me help you."

For a moment, hysteria threatened in Beth's eyes. Then she controlled herself and let Ashley help her to the sofa. Ashley got a pillow and wrapped blankets around her mother. She got a warm rag and gently wiped a trickle of blood from the corner of Beth's mouth, then kissed her on the forehead. More than two hours had passed by the time Ashley finally slumped back into bed.

After a few troubled hours of sleep, it was time to get up and ready for school. Ashley dragged herself into a warm shower, awakened her two school-aged siblings, fed them breakfast and got their lunches ready. When the baby cried, she changed his diaper and gave him a bottle of milk to keep him occupied. Before leaving with her sisters to catch the corner bus, Ashley peeked in on her sleeping father and placed a feather-light kiss on her mother's swollen, purple cheek. Then she turned to face the new day.

All day in school Ashley worried over what might be going on at home. Would Dad be mean when he woke up? Would Mom need to go to the doctor? Would they be able to care for the baby? Would Dad hurt him?

What's Going on at Home?

For some time, Ashley's fifth-grade teacher has suspected something amiss in the girl's home life. Ashley is a smart, capable student; yet, on many days she seems completely preoccupied. Her teacher refrains from broaching the subject with Ashley or her parents. Beth seems aloof at parent-teacher conferences and Ashley is very protective and guarded about her home life. The teacher is half afraid to know what might be going on. She justifies her lack of involvement by convincing herself that she might be opening a can of worms she probably couldn't do anything about, anyway.

For Ashley's part, she wishes deep inside that someone could just know about her parents' problems and miraculously help her family. But Ashley doesn't think this will happen—so she just lives with incessant worries about what goes on at home when she's away and about what she will find when she gets there.

Unspoken Anxieties

Children of alcoholics, like Ashley, may worry over what's going on at home when they are away at school, at friends' homes, outside playing or even when they are asleep. Children who are old enough to voice their concerns usually don't because:

1. They are afraid of repercussions from their parents

2. They don't want to burden their already troubled parents

3. They doubt that anyone would believe their stories or do anything about them anyway

4. They feel like traitors even thinking of telling someone outside the family about personal problems

5. They may not realize that the way they live is abnormal.

The anxieties of children who are too young to know or tell what is bothering them often come out in the form of headaches, stomachaches, nightmares, or refusal to participate in activities that take them away from home. These children struggle blindly in an attempt to bring their lives onto a "normal" course. They may not consciously know what normal is or what they're struggling for, but they have an innate sense that something is very wrong.

The Character Shredder

Darryl Johnson is a hard-driving, ambitious man who exacts a lot from his subordinates at work and his family at home. He is an alcoholic and has abused his wife, Mary, both mentally and physically, for more than fifteen years. Their son, Tom, is eleven years old and their daughter, Stephanie, is nine. Mary relates a "typical" scenario to a counselor at the Crisis Shelter for Battered Wives:

"Darryl came home from work drunk. Before we ever got to the dinner table he had slapped Tom for leaving his bike on the front lawn and hollered at Stephanie for forgetting her dolls on the living room sofa. He tried to seduce me in the kitchen as I was preparing dinner. I rejected his advances and hoped desperately that he would pass out watching television after he ate. I guess my turning him away wounded his pride, and he began calling me awful names and shouting that a man should be able to expect some reward for his hard work at the office!"

Mary's face contorts into a half-grimace, half-sneer. "I despise him when he says things like that! I work full-time in an office. My salary actually supports our family. Darryl's money pretty much supports his drinking and supplements my income.

"Anyway, by the time we were seated at the table last

night, I was afraid that Darryl was going to let loose on one of us. I guess I should have just gone to bed with him and tried to avoid what happened."

Mary's face droops in a pitiful, grief-stricken expression. "Poor Tom—he accidentally spilled his milk, and Darryl lit into him something awful! Tom sat there like a brave soldier and listened to his father call him a clumsy, irresponsible idiot and a stupid, inconsiderate loser. Tom stared right through Darryl but his hands were fisted so tight in front of him that his knuckles were white. It is truly sick that such a small incident can get blown out of proportion so badly, but that has gotten to be an almost daily occurrence at our house."

As Mary gets deeper into the telling of the evening's events, she assumes a posture of shame. She hangs her head as she continues, "Tom learned long ago not to speak one word when Darryl is drunk. But that doesn't always pacify Darryl. It didn't last night. Darryl started badgering Tom. 'C'mon, big man—speak up! What do you have to say to your old man about this? Huh? Huh? C'mon!' I don't know what Tom could possibly have said. What is there to say when you spill a glass of milk and someone rips your entire character apart?"

Mary grips the arms of her chair as she forces herself to come to the crux of what happened. "Tom remained silent and before I knew it, Darryl pulled him up out of his chair by one arm and slammed him to the floor. Darryl bellowed at him, 'You little s-of-a-b, answer me!' I screamed and jumped up to help Tom. That enraged Darryl even more. He backhanded me so hard that I fell over. He grabbed Tom again. Tom was sobbing and kicking. I don't know how far it would've gone because the phone rang. Thankfully, something changed directions in Darryl's mind. He growled at me to answer the phone and he stomped out of the house and left in the car.

"I let the phone ring and went to the kids. Tom was scrunched into a ball on the floor, holding his arm and howling like an animal caught in a trap. Stephanie was sitting at her place at the table looking at her plate. I think she blocks the scenes out of her conscious mind sometimes in order to survive them. Things like this have happened before. We never know when they'll come, what will trigger them or how bad they'll get!"

Mary does not appear to notice that tears are streaming down her face or that she is rocking back and forth. She says she has lived with this long enough and she's got to do something but she doesn't know what. She feels that she has nowhere to turn and doubts her own capabilities to provide for her children by herself.

"If I've put up with Darryl's drinking and violence for all these years there must be something terribly wrong with me! I don't know if I trust myself to change our lives around! But the poor kids—" Mary's eyes fill with horror and she sobs painfully. "My poor children!"

Mary and Darryl obviously have a multitude of problems that should be confronted and dealt with. Unfortunately for Tom and Stephanie, and for many other children in alcoholic homes, confrontations and problem solving often come too late or not at all. Wounds are carved deep into the tender hearts, gentle souls or young bodies of children long before there's anything done about the destruction caused by alcoholism in the family—if anything is *ever* done about it.

Wounded Bodies, Crushed Souls

Tammy tried to escape the troubles of her alcoholic home by turning to a boyfriend. She says, "When I was fifteen I got pregnant, ran away from home, had an abortion, and nearly died from complications afterward. That was ten years ago but I remember it as if it were yesterday. At the time, I thought that I was the dirtiest, most sinful girl alive. I look back and see that my mother's alcoholism was too much for me to bear and it catapulted me into an unhealthy search for love. I was cooking, cleaning and caring for my mother before I went to junior high school. I can't remember a time when she wasn't drinking. I have two older brothers who did not seem to notice or care about Mom's drinking. I took sole responsibility for being a champion to my mother's 'cause.' When I think about the arguments my parents used to have and all the stress I lived with, it's no wonder I ran into the arms of the first boy that showed me any affection. There just wasn't any unconditional love in our home. When I got pregnant, I panicked. The boy didn't want anything to do with me. I took his rejection in stride, however, because I was used to rejection.

"For instance, there were times when I would come home from school and quickly put things in order, hoping that I could make things be all right. What I usually got for my efforts was my mother causing a scene at the dinner table about my not getting to the store for a gallon of milk, hearing that I just couldn't do anything right and my parents ending up in a fight! There was no way I could turn to my parents for help with my pregnancy.

"I took money from my father's wallet one evening, knowing he'd blame my mother for spending it. The next morning I left for school as usual and went right to a free clinic that was advertised in the yellow pages of a phone book, had an abortion, and was released onto the sidewalk a couple hours later. I felt pretty woozy so I walked to a fast-food restaurant. I must have started hemorrhaging and passed out. The next thing I remember is waking up in a hospital bed with a pastor patting my hand."

Tammy's parents were contacted that evening by the pastor, Reverend Morris, and arrangements were made for them to take her home the next day. When he went to Tammy a short while later he had a sad, sympathetic expression on his face. He spoke softly to her. "Our time together will be brief, Tammy. I want you to try to relax and talk to me in all honesty about your situation. Tell me how you came to be pregnant at fifteen and why you felt you had to run away for an abortion. What's it like at home, Tammy?"

Tammy's eyes swell with tears even now as she speaks. "It was the first time I remember anyone caring about why I did anything or what I was going through. I guess I couldn't hold it in any longer because I kept Reverend Morris up well into the night telling him my life story. Unburdening all those years of pain, guilt, frustration, anger, hatred, responsibility and confusion was a huge relief. You know, the children of alcoholics are like alarm clocks that are wound too tight from the beginning. They wind down, year by year, with no one there to rewind them. Either their springs snap in the middle like mine did with my teen pregnancy, running away and having an abortion, or they go on with life until they give in to some other kind of collapse."

Reverend Morris listened quietly to Tammy's story. Then he shook his head. "Tammy, I only have these few hours with you before you go home to your parents. I'm going to try very hard to give you enough seeds of knowledge and hope about God to make you want to seek out His guidance in your life from now on.

"In our short time together, Tammy, I cannot possibly help you get over the pain of growing up with alcoholism, but the Lord can. Go to Him and He will help you—He will love you more than you can imagine!"

When a nurse brought Tammy her breakfast tray at seven o'clock, Reverend Morris' head was nodding as he slept sitting in the chair at the side of the bed. Tammy was staring out the window. She turned to the nurse and said, "I don't want to wake him up because I'm afraid he'll leave."

The nurse said kindly, "He won't mind if you let him sleep, and I know that he'll stay with you as long as he can."

Tammy only picked at the food on her tray. Reverend Morris woke up a short while later. He spoke briefly with Tammy about her going home and warned her that she shouldn't think things would change much with her parents right away—maybe they'd always be the way they were. He said he would make arrangements for her to attend Alateen meetings for young people with alcoholic parents and see that a pastor friend of his in her city contacted Tammy about counseling.

By the time Tammy's parents came to get her at noon, Reverend Morris had planted several seeds of hope within her soul. One of the seeds that was already sprouting was Reverend Morris's assurance that God was NOT like human parents—He would not disappoint her!

Members of alcoholic family networks, like Tammy, Joshua, Ashley, Blake, Beth, Darryl, Mary, Tom, and Stephanie, desperately need seeds of hope—hope that their lives can be more than long paths of disappointments and upheavals.

Hebrews 6:19 speaks of a hope that is an anchor for the soul. Members of alcoholic family networks can grasp that anchor and hope to rise above mere survival, believing that they can move onward to full, successful lives.

Where to Get More Information

Al-Anon/Alateen Family Group Headquarters, Inc.
Madison Square Station
New York, New York 10010
Alcoholics Anonymous World Service, Inc.
468 Park Avenue South
New York, New York 10016
(212) 686-1100
National Association for Children of Alcoholics
31706 Coast Highway, Suite 201
South Laguna, California 92677
(714) 499-3889
National Clearinghouse for Alcohol Information
P. O. Box 1908
Rockville, Maryland 20850
(301) 468-2600
National Council on Alcoholism
12 West 21st Street
New York, New York 10010
(212) 206-6770

National Federation of Drug-Free Youth
8730 Georgia Avenue
Suite 200
Silver Spring, Maryland 20910
National Institute on Drug Abuse
5600 Fishers Lane
Rockville, Maryland 20857
Overcomers Outreach, Inc.
2290 West Whittier Boulevard
Suite A/D
La Habra, California 90631
(213) 697-3994

SUGGESTED READING

Black, Claudia. *It Will Never Happen to Me*. Denver: Medical Administration Company, 1982.
Brooks, C. *The Secret Everyone Knows*. San Diego: The Kroc Foundation, 1981.
Drews, Toby R. *Getting Them Sober*. South Plainfield, NJ: Bridge Publishings, Inc., 1980.
Greenleaf, Jael. *Co-Alcoholic—Para-Alcoholic: Who's Who and What's the Difference?*. Los Angeles: MAC Publishers, 1981.
Gravitz, Herbert L. and Bowden, Julie D. *Recovery: A Guide for Adult Children of Alcoholics*. Holmes Beach, FL: Learning Publications, Inc., 1985.
Martin, Sara Hines. *Healing for Adult Children of Alcoholics*. Nashville: Broadman Press, 1988.
Milam, James R. and Ketcham, Katherine. *Under the Influence: A Guide to the Myths and Realities of Alcoholism*. Seattle: Madrona Publishers, Inc., 1981.
Wegschieder, Sharon. *Another Chance: Hope and Health*

for the Alcoholic Family. Palo Alto, CA: Science and Behavior Books, 1981.
Woititz, Janet G. *Adult Children of Alcoholics.* Hollywood, FL: Health Communications, Inc., 1983.
—————. *Marriage on the Rocks.* New York: Delacorte Press, 1979.
For additional reading, look in the card catalog in your local library under the following subject headings:
Alcohol
Alcoholics
Adult Children of Alcoholics
Family Relationships